# There's Three in Our Marriage: My Spouse, Me, and Technology

*A Guide to Getting a Handle on the Overuse of Technology at Home*

Sandy Wright

# Table of Contents

INTRODUCTION ....................................................................................1

CHAPTER 1: UNDERSTANDING THE DIGITAL DISCONNECT .................7

    *Dysfunctional Communication* ........................................................8
    *Distraction* ...................................................................................9
    *Social Pressure* ............................................................................9
    *Invasion of Privacy* ......................................................................9
    *Mistrust* .....................................................................................10
    *Emotional Disconnect* ................................................................10
  RECOGNIZING SIGNS OF TECHNOLOGY OVERUSE ............................11
    *Laxity* ........................................................................................11
    *Isolation* ....................................................................................12
    *Hiding in Plain Sight* ..................................................................12
    *Anxiety* ......................................................................................12
  IDENTIFYING THE REASONS BEHIND EXCESSIVE TECH HABITS ............13
    *The Oblivious Pawn* ...................................................................14
    *Escape from Reality* ...................................................................14
  TECH'S TOLL ON YOUR MARRIAGE, FAMILY, AND EMOTIONAL CONNECTION ...................15
    *Intimacy* ....................................................................................16
    *Communication Challenges* ........................................................16
    *Satisfaction* ...............................................................................16
    *Disconnection from Reality* ........................................................17

CHAPTER 2: THE EFFECT ON YOUR RELATIONSHIP ..........................19

  HONEY, WE HAVE A PROBLEM! ....................................................20
  EXPLORE THE EMOTIONAL DISCONNECT ........................................23
  TECHNOLOGY ROBS YOU OF QUALITY TIME AND INTIMACY .............25
  EFFECT ON THE KIDS ...................................................................27

CHAPTER 3: LEADING BY EXAMPLE................................................29

  ASSESSING YOUR TECH HABITS ....................................................31
    *Your Own Tech Use* ...................................................................32
    *Compulsive Use* .........................................................................33
  MODELING HEALTHY TECH USE THROUGH SELF-REGULATION ...........34
  STRONGER THROUGH MUTUAL EFFORTS ......................................36
    *Usage Limits* ..............................................................................37
    *Push Notifications* ......................................................................37

*A Fresh Start* ...................................................................... *37*

*Be Intentional* ................................................................... *38*

*Mindful Tech Use* .............................................................. *38*

**CHAPTER 4: NAVIGATING TECHNOLOGY BOUNDARIES** ............................**41**

*Setting Boundaries* ........................................................... *42*

YOUR SPOUSE ISN'T ON BOARD YET... WHAT NEXT? ........................42

TIPS FOR SETTING HEALTHY TECH USE BOUNDARIES IN YOUR RELATIONSHIP ...............46

*Why Boundaries Help* ...................................................... *46*

NEGOTIATING MUTUALLY ACCEPTABLE GUIDELINES FOR DEVICE USAGE ...............48

*Tech-Free Time* ................................................................ *49*

*Avoid Comparisons* .......................................................... *49*

*Teachable Moments* ......................................................... *50*

**CHAPTER 5: FINDING BALANCE IN THE DIGITAL WORLD** .................**53**

SHARED ACTIVITY WITHOUT TECHNOLOGY.....................................55

QUALITY TIME .......................................................................57

*Personal Quality Time* ..................................................... *58*

*The Power of Surprises* .................................................... *60*

*Reconnect Through Shared Experiences* ............................ *60*

*Relive the Treasure* .......................................................... *61*

*Relax and Pamper Each Other* .......................................... *62*

**CHAPTER 6: CULTIVATING EMOTIONAL INTIMACY** ...........................**63**

THE ROLE OF EMOTIONAL INTIMACY IN A HEALTHY RELATIONSHIP.................66

*It's Good for Your Confidence* ........................................... *67*

*Be Honest With One Another* ............................................ *67*

*Multifaceted Growth* ....................................................... *68*

PRACTICING ACTIVE LISTENING AND EMPATHY..............................68

*The Role of Listening and Empathy* ................................... *69*

**CHAPTER 7: OVERCOMING TECHNOLOGY ADDICTION** ......................**73**

RECOGNIZING THE IMPACT OF ADDICTION ON YOUR RELATIONSHIP ...............77

*Behavioral Changes*.......................................................... *77*

*Communication Challenges* .............................................. *78*

*Emotional Changes*........................................................... *78*

*Disrupted Quality Time*..................................................... *79*

SUPPORTING YOUR SPOUSE IN THEIR JOURNEY TO REDUCE RELIANCE ON TECH.................80

*Sharing What You've Noticed*............................................. *80*

*Empathetic Communication* .............................................. *81*

SEEKING PROFESSIONAL HELP AND RESOURCES.............................82

*Embrace Your Reality* ....................................................... *82*

*Discuss Options*................................................................ *83*

*Honest Communication* ..................................................... *83*

Book Appointments ................................................................83

Do the Work ........................................................................83

**CHAPTER 8: REKINDLING ROMANCE AND INTIMACY ........................85**

Immediate Family ................................................................86

Significant Other ................................................................86

Friends ..............................................................................87

WORKING THROUGH LOST TRUST ...........................................88

Reach Out ...........................................................................88

Separate the Person From the Addiction ...............................89

Reasonable Expectations .....................................................89

Utmost Honesty ..................................................................89

Move Forward .....................................................................90

Reconnect ...........................................................................90

REIGNITING PASSION AND ROMANCE IN THE DIGITAL AGE .............91

Hold Hands .........................................................................91

Thrill-seeking .....................................................................91

Outdoorsy Activities ...........................................................92

WAYS TO PRIORITIZE PHYSICAL AND EMOTIONAL CLOSENESS ........93

**CHAPTER 9: IMPROVING COMMUNICATION IN A TECH-DOMINATED WORLD ..97**

Open-Ended Conversations ..................................................98

Nonverbal Cues ..................................................................99

Reading Minds ...................................................................100

Mutual Effort ....................................................................100

NAVIGATING CONFLICTS RELATED TO TECHNOLOGY USE ..............101

ENHANCE COMMUNICATION THROUGH MINDFUL USE OF TECHNOLOGY ...........103

STRENGTHEN EMOTIONAL BONDS THROUGH TRANSPARENT COMMUNICATION .............104

**CHAPTER 10: CONNECTING WITH OTHERS FOR SUPPORT .............107**

Communication Breakdown ...............................................108

Broken Trust .....................................................................109

You're Living Like Roomies ...............................................109

For the Kids ......................................................................110

SUPPORT FROM FRIENDS AND FAMILY ...................................111

SUPPORT GROUPS AND THERAPY ...........................................113

Couples Therapy ...............................................................113

**CHAPTER 11: THE WAY FORWARD: EMBRACING A BALANCED TECH-LIFE MARRIAGE ..................................................................121**

REFLECTING ON PROGRESS IN YOUR JOURNEY ..........................123

Actively Support Each Other ..............................................125

Date Your Spouse Like You're Still Courting ........................125

Rediscover the First Impressions ........................................126

CELEBRATING SUCCESS AND OVERCOMING CHALLENGES TOGETHER ..............................126
Where Do You Go From Here?........................................................................127
ONGOING COMMITMENT TO A THRIVING RELATIONSHIP..............................................129
Emotional Intimacy and Safety.....................................................................129
Mutual Support and Growth .......................................................................129
Security and Trust......................................................................................130
Shared Memories and Experiences...............................................................130

**CONCLUSION** .................................................................................................**133**

**REFERENCES**..................................................................................................**137**

# Introduction

Relationships change everything. Whether you're married, engaged, dating, or in any other kind of relationship, you're sharing your life with someone. Spending so much time with that person can shape your perspective on a lot of things, especially your approach to life.

Relationships are like business spouseships. A spouseship is formed when two or more people come together and are committed to pursuing common objectives. What this means is that despite their unique differences, spouses agree to work toward achieving the common objectives of their spouseship. In many cases, spouseships thrive by virtue of the members' differences, in that everyone brings a different perspective or way of doing things to the table, and by doing so, they come up with various solutions to tackle challenges.

Now, let's take this back to relationships. In the framework of a spouseship, you and your spouse are two individuals with different personalities and perspectives on life. Even if you share a lot of similarities, there will always be some fundamental differences. Despite these differences, you share similar objectives for the relationship. You want to grow old together, make some investments, travel the world, and so on.

All these objectives are achievable. We both know a lot of couples that have done it. One of the key ingredients for such long-lasting relationships is effective communication, but that's where things get murky.

Most people assume that communication is all about talking to your spouse or listening to what they're saying. While that is true, there's so much more to communication. At times, silence between couples communicates much more than the spoken word.

1

One of the challenges plaguing communication in relationships is that we take a lot for granted. We assume things, and that's when we start drifting away from each other. In the modern age, communication is one of the key pillars of successful relationships that suffers in the face of technology.

Sure, we text and call each other all the time, but do we really communicate?

You find yourself in an even more precarious position when your spouse is addicted to their tech gadgets. It could be anything from their phone to their laptop, or even their video games. While this might not have bothered you at all from the onset, it's become a big problem because you're suddenly worlds apart. Perhaps, when it started, you let it slide because you felt it was good to give your spouse space to just be themselves and enjoy the things they love doing, independent of you. However, as this went on, you grew apart, so much so that at times it felt like your spouse would rather be immersed in their gadgets than spend time with you.

This scenario might not capture how you ended up in this predicament, but it is something that many people go through in their relationships. You've been ignored and unheard, and are playing second fiddle to your spouse's tech, and that's not okay.

It's quite heartbreaking, especially when you consider that there was once a time when you were inseparable. There was a time in your relationship when all you needed was a glance at each other and a message would have been communicated, quite clearly, to be precise. Today, you walk into the room and your spouse has a conversation with you without ever lifting their eyes off their devices. It's like they're not even there.

The unfortunate thing about this predicament is that it's become so common that it's been normalized in some relationships. That shouldn't be the case.

While our devices have become part and parcel of our lives, excessive use has created lots of problems in relationships. Face-to-face communication is the first thing that flies out the window. The more your spouse immerses themselves in these devices, the harder it gets for you to share meaningful conversations. Exchanges you used to look forward to suddenly become reduced to one-word responses. Instead of engaging discussions, your interactions are reduced to giving and receiving instructions.

When your conversations are no longer engaging, you start missing out on quality time. You long for the days when the biggest confrontation you had was who was going to be the big spoon when you cuddled on the sofa. Instead, such shared experiences and bonding opportunities have been replaced by screens. You don't even watch the same shows anymore. If you're watching something on Netflix in the living room, your spouse is catching up on their favorite show either on their phone or on the TV in the bedroom.

Once quality time is gone, intimacy can then be affected. The physical and emotional connection gradually dissipates to a point where you start wondering whether your spouse is getting attention from someone else. These days, they barely notice that you changed your hair, or that you're using a new perfume. These are the simple things that we take for granted, yet for relationships, they make the biggest difference.

As your connection withers, a vacuum is created in your relationship. In most cases, that vacuum is occupied by misunderstandings, fights, and trust issues. That's the thing about relationships—they should never have space for a vacuum. If you allow one to happen, you can never tell, or control, what occupies that vacuum.

Technology isn't the first place where you and your spouse's opinions vary. You want to shop at Walmart, they'd rather go to Target. You'd rather go out to a restaurant, but they'd rather order in and have the items delivered. You've had these conversations before. However, the difference is that earlier on in the relationship, compromise was easier. You'd weigh both options and decide whether to shop online or not. You'd even decide which items to get from Walmart and which to get from Target. The day you stepped out to shop together, you looked forward to it. Today, such a simple discussion becomes so charged that you wonder why you even bothered to ask in the first place.

The increase in confrontations in your relationship deals a severe blow to your trust. Your spouse is always on their phone, so it's only natural that at some point, you'll start questioning whether they're talking to or seeing someone else. They seem happier when chatting away on their phone than they are when talking to you. Your very presence seems like a distraction, a bother, something they'd rather get done with fast so they can go back to their devices. Your spouse might not even be talking to someone; maybe they're just deeply immersed in their video games. However, the neglect gets to you, and at such a point, no one would blame you for being jealous.

You get frustrated. Resentment kicks in. You feel lonely and isolated from your spouse. Eventually, you start wondering whether the relationship is worth fighting for. You don't have proof that your spouse is cheating on you, but the neglect is too much. You don't recognize the person you're living with anymore. Even worse, you barely recognize yourself.

This is the point where self-doubt comes in. You start questioning why you allow yourself this much disrespect. You remember the days when you'd walk away from a relationship in a heartbeat if you ever went through something like this. Luckily, you're not in that frame of mind anymore. You're committed to this relationship and, despite the challenges, you want it to work.

Addiction to tech suffocates your relationship by placing it in an unyielding stranglehold. It eats away at the foundation of your spouseship until it gets to a point where you can barely recognize each other. For some people, tech can be an easy escape from addressing the issues plaguing their relationship. This, perhaps, could be what your spouse is going through. However, escapism doesn't solve anything. Relationship issues are best addressed when you work together to find lasting solutions.

All is not lost. Despite what you might feel sometimes, there's hope for your relationship. You can bring back the good old days and have the loving, caring, and supportive relationship you once had.

I won't lie to you and say it's going to be a walk in the park. No. This is going to be hard work. However, I can assure you that if you work on this together with your spouse, you'll emerge on the other side confident, stronger, and more committed to one another than before.

I say this because working on your spouse's tech addiction will reveal a lot of truths about your relationship. It could be quite an eye opener, reminding you of what you once had, and shining a light on where you are today.

Working through this will involve bringing back the power of open, honest, and loving communication with one another. You'll learn not just the importance of boundaries in relationships, but more importantly, how to set and enforce them.

This will be a wholesome journey, because even though you set out to help your spouse overcome their tech addiction and find their way back to you, the lessons you'll pick up from this will go a long way toward reaffirming your commitment to one another. Through this journey, you'll re-learn the value of quality time and prioritizing one another. You'll become self-aware, recognizing where your own tech habits could have led to some of the challenges you're experiencing in your relationship.

Finally, it's crucial to understand that technology, in itself, is not a danger to your relationship. If anything, there are many ways that technology could rejuvenate your relationship. The problem with technology is the way we use it in the relationship. At the end of the day, it's the people in the relationship who make it or break it.

# Chapter 1:

# Understanding the Digital

# Disconnect

*They are so caught up in their happiness that they don't realize I'm not really a part of it. I am wandering along the periphery. I am like the people in the Winslow Homer paintings, sharing the same room with them but not really there.*

*I am like the fish in the aquarium, thinking in a different language, adapting to a life that's not my natural habitat. I am the people in the other cars, each with his or her own story, but passing too quickly to be noticed or understood.*

*. . . There are moments I just sit in my frame, float in my tank, ride in my car and say nothing, think nothing that connects me to anything at all.* — David Levithan

The problem has been going on for a while. You've tried to rise above it, but it's become so apparent that you cannot ignore it anymore. It's eating away at your inner peace. You feel like a stranger all the time. You have moments when you feel unwanted. How did you become this person? How did you get to this point?

You've probably pondered these questions more times than you'd wish to admit, but this is your reality now. You're living through a relationship that you can barely recognize. At one time, you longed for the moments you'd spend with your spouse. You cherished those moments because they were perfect.

You remember the days when you'd spend time together and feel like the whole world stopped and you were the only two people who mattered. Everything was bliss and a pocketful of sunshine. Those days seem like a distant memory because you can barely recognize the person you're living with anymore.

Even when you and your spouse are alone, the space feels too crowded with everyone else but you. What kind of life is this?

Unfortunately, this is the life that many people are going through. Feeling like a stranger in your relationship, in your house, is one of the worst things that could ever happen to anyone who's in a committed relationship. Yet, the culprit isn't someone you can talk to and ask to stay away. The culprit is a choice, one that your spouse makes every day.

Technology has been a disrupting force in many industries in the past decade. Tech is all around us, changing the way we do things. We have the likes of Uber, Airbnb, and OpenAI making significant strides in transforming the way we go about our lives, and that can be beautiful. Unfortunately, the disruptive force of technology is a double-edged sword. The swiftness and effectiveness with which tech is disrupting industries is also killing relationships.

Technology is efficient. That is one aspect that makes it a powerful element in our lives. Therefore, when it disrupts your relationship, you can be certain that the outcome will be quite efficient. I mean, you're living through the impact right now. Your spouse's dalliance with their devices is wrecking your relationship and you're now at a point where you no longer feel loved around them.

Addiction to devices is just as detrimental as drug addiction. Your spouse is so hooked on their devices that they barely recognize your presence. In some instances, your presence almost feels like a bother. Let's explore some challenges that a spouse's tech addiction could impose on relationships. You might find some or all of them relatable.

## *Dysfunctional Communication*

You once had a peaceful, harmonious relationship. However, this has been replaced by frequent bickering and misunderstandings. Your spouse is often hooked on their screens, texting and scrolling away. You can barely get to them and if you do, your conversations are curt and lack the empathy that you were used to. Without the nuances of face-to-face interaction, your conversations are easily misinterpreted, hence the misunderstandings you've been experiencing from time to time.

## Distraction

Your spouse seems distracted when you're talking to them. Their gadgets seem to get in the way of your conversations. Even when you want to spend some quality time with them, perhaps watch a movie together, you can barely make it through a few minutes before they pick up their phone to see what the latest notification is all about. This kind of distraction makes you feel unimportant, unloved, and neglected.

## Social Pressure

If your spouse is hooked on social media, there's a good chance you're struggling to keep up with the social pressure. Social media creates friction in relationships because for some reason, your spouse might be trying to live up to unrealistic standards.

Just because some strangers online are doing things a certain way doesn't mean you must also comply. Yet your spouse doesn't seem to realize this. Instead, they keep comparing your lives to the seemingly perfect lives that other people are showing online.

The challenge here is that in most cases, those social media experiences aren't real. People barely reveal or live their real lives online. Behind all the filters and perfectly edited photos, videos and stories, everyone else is just living a normal, simple life. Unfortunately, your spouse doesn't realize this, and their persistence leaves you feeling dissatisfied and inadequate.

## Invasion of Privacy

Your home is meant to be your sanctuary. It is your safe place, as was your spouse once upon a time. Unfortunately, their persistence in staying constantly connected to the digital world makes you feel like a stranger in a space that was once your safety nest. You're feeling suffocated because everywhere you turn, you find a device connected to the digital world. Your spouse might also be feeling suffocated because everywhere they turn, you seem to be asking them to disconnect.

## Mistrust

One of the challenges of tech addiction is that it creates an aspect of mistrust in the relationship. Since your spouse is constantly connected to their devices, you start wondering whether they're talking to someone else behind your back. They might not be doing so, but something about the shift in their energy whenever you come into their space leaves you wondering whether they've found someone else.

None of this is helped by the fact that connecting with strangers online is so easy these days. All it takes is a single conversation and you go down the rabbit hole. This is how people end up in secret online relationships and emotional affairs that cause more harm to their real relationships than they know.

## Emotional Disconnect

Instead of talking to one another, your relationship now revolves around texting. Sure, there was a time when texting was awesome. Your shared messages were well-thought-out, and you could feel the love in them. Today, however, your messages are brief, and mostly filled with instructions.

Texting might be convenient, but it lacks the emotional connection of face-to-face conversations. Some conversations are best had in person than conveyed over text messages. One of the problems of texting is that it does not capture the context of the engagement, leaving too much room for misinterpretation.

If you're reading this book, you're probably living through some or all of the concerns we've raised above. They're eating away at the fabric of your relationship. You might have moments when you wonder whether the relationship is worth saving at all. You've carried the burden for so long that you wonder whether your spouse is still in the relationship with you.

Excessive use of technology creates a deep disconnect in the relationship that many couples struggle to come back from. Relationships are meant to be full of shared experiences, but yours isn't. Instead, you're living with someone who would rather spend time on their devices than immerse themselves in real-world experiences with you.

What makes this absence worse is that your spouse wasn't always like that. They used to enjoy the real world with you. You used to do so many things together, but right now, you feel like you're asking too much of them if you just want to spend a few minutes together. This is how addiction to tech strangles the emotional connection in relationships.

# Recognizing Signs of Technology Overuse

Your relationship is struggling, or at least you think it is. You have noticed that your spouse is spending too much time on their devices, but how can you be certain that you are not overreacting? One of the worst things to do in a relationship is usually to act on a whim, only to realize that you were wrong. Complaining about tech use is quite an accusation, so before you confront your spouse about it, be sure that you are right. The question, therefore, is how do you confirm that your spouse's puttering around with their tech is overuse, and not just a random thing? How much is too much? The last thing you want to do is create a problem where there was none in the first place.

To be fair, there's no defined amount of time someone should spend on their devices to be considered an addict. For relationships, you might have clearly defined usage times, so the problem arises when these are breached. For example, you could have a rule about no gadgets in the bedroom, or no devices at the dinner table. When your spouse ignores this, then you need to talk about it. That aside, the easiest way to identify a tech addict is to recognize changes in their behavior patterns. What follows are some signs that could indicate misuse, or overuse.

## Laxity

Does your spouse get things done on time? Think about it. How often do they struggle to complete their chores, or any other task that they were supposed to? Do you often have to pick up on their chores, remind them, or simply demand that they put their devices down and get some work done? If that's the case, there's a good chance your spouse is addicted to their devices. It could be the phone, video games, or anything else, but it's taking too much of their time and energy, so this needs to be addressed.

## Isolation

How would you describe your social life? Does your spouse suddenly prefer to spend as little time as possible with friends and family members? This could be a sign of an addiction. The problem is particularly noticeable when you realize that you no longer spend as much time together as you used to. Even worse, when your spouse can't focus when you're hanging out because they're constantly checking their phone or some other tech, this might be a sign that they would rather be anywhere else than where you are.

## Hiding in Plain Sight

Sometimes, an addict knows when they are doing the wrong thing. The guilt eats away at their conscience, and as a result, they try to conceal their tech use from you or anyone else who might call them out on their behavior. For example, let's say your spouse spends too much time on their phone. If you've had the conversation about it before, your spouse is fully aware of your displeasure. As a result, they'll try to sneak away to a quiet place in the house to use their phone. This is a sign of a problem. Apart from that, your spouse might get irritated and angry if you happen to walk in on them using their phone while in hiding, or if you interrupt them.

## Anxiety

Notice how your spouse behaves when they cannot access their phone for some reason. Perhaps they forgot it in the car, or at home, or the battery runs out right in the middle of something they were quite invested in. These are signs that they have an unhealthy relationship with their phone, and you need to talk about it.

They may also have a constant compulsion to check their devices, even when they have no real need to do so. A common phenomenon is the phantom vibration. This is a situation where your spouse thinks their phone is vibrating, even when it's not. It might even be someone else's phone, but your spouse will still check theirs just in case.

Nothing's wrong with checking your phone or devices from time to time. It becomes a problem when your spouse invests too much of their time, to the point where it disrupts their work, relationships, and other important things in their life. If any of these describe the situation in your relationship, then you need to take proactive measures to fight back for your relationship.

## Identifying the Reasons Behind Excessive Tech Habits

Let's go behind the scenes. You've already noticed the glaring signs that your spouse's tech use is unhealthy. Initially, it might have been a hunch, but the facts are clear right now. You're struggling to understand why they can't just spend time with you or your kids without feeling the need to check their phone from time to time. What's so important in that phone that would take their attention from the things and people who matter?

In this section, we try to understand why your spouse is spending a lot of time on their devices. Unfortunately, this puts you in a burdensome position. On one hand, you are not getting the attention you deserve from your spouse, and your needs have been neglected for a while. On the other hand, you must now try to understand why your spouse, who doesn't seem to realize they're wrecking your relationship, is doing what they're doing.

Here's the thing about technology that most people never realize—it's designed to distract you. Well, most of it is. Let's explore this.

## *The Oblivious Pawn*

Tech companies spend a lot of money to get one thing in return, your attention. They have pumped billions of dollars into research and experiments to understand human psychology. Therefore, your spouse is addicted to their devices not by chance, but by design. These companies try to learn as much as possible about your likes and dislikes, hobbies, and so on. Then they create products that deliver everything you desire, right at your fingertips. Unfortunately, people are wired differently, so not all of us are strong enough to fight back and deny ourselves the satisfaction.

Why do tech companies want your attention so badly? Why do they go out of their way to keep you hooked on their products? The answer is quite simple: It's all about the money!

As long as they have your attention, they can sell it to advertisers, who similarly need that attention. This is why you constantly see ads that seem relatable. For example, when you've just welcomed a newborn into the household, you're probably seeing a lot of ads about baby products, wellness, and other things that are relevant in your household at the moment. As soon as you join the gym, you'll suddenly see more ads about gym and nutrition products. None of this is a coincidence. Someone's spending tons of money to try to sell you something. What this means is that your spouse could be just another pawn in a bigger game that they might not even realize they are playing.

## *Escape from Reality*

Another reason why your spouse might be so drawn to their tech is because they get to temporarily escape from their reality. We've all been there. We have such a difficult day at work that all we need is to get away from it all. We all have different realities and we process things differently. Perhaps your spouse just needed an escape from the stress they go through in life, in the relationship, or for any other reason, and they gradually got sucked down the rabbit hole.

Going back to the previous point on distraction by design, tech offers an immediate escape. The simplest way to avoid your problems is to distract yourself with something else, and tech offers just that. Instead of talking about what's bothering them, your spouse sought solace in their phone, video game, or any other gadget that's now threatening the peace and harmony in your relationship.

Did you know that tech companies are not compelled to issue warnings or take proactive measures to protect users from the impact of distraction caused by their devices? Some companies have gone ahead and done that, but that's of their own volition, not because they are legally required to do so. At the end of the day, healthy use of tech is your responsibility.

When you realize that your spouse is suddenly spending more time on their devices than seems healthy for them, you should talk to them about it, try to figure out what they are running away from. Most often, it's an opportunity to escape from something. Get to the bottom of it.

# Tech's Toll on Your Marriage, Family, and Emotional Connection

You've recognized the signs, explored possible reasons why your spouse might be deeply hooked on their devices, and now you need to have that difficult conversation you've been dreading. After all, your spouse doesn't seem to realize how bad off the relationship is. To them, everything seems to be working smoothly, business as usual.

The time has come to address the effects of this problem on your relationship. This is not to accuse your spouse, but to help them have an open and honest conversation with you about the situation at hand. The issues might not be apparent yet, and your spouse might not even realize they exist, but in the long run, living in their devices exerts a toll on your marriage and family, and you become emotionally estranged.

How do you have this conversation? Let's say you have your spouse's attention. What kind of issues should you raise? The time they're spending on their devices is obviously a concern, but what next? Here are some things you can bring to their attention to help them understand the struggle your relationship is going through.

## Intimacy

Relationships experience a lot of challenges, so ups and downs from time to time are not uncommon. However, explain to your spouse why you feel you've been intimately distant since they started spending more time on their tech.

## Communication Challenges

Talk to your spouse about the sudden change in the way you communicate with one another. You might have noticed a difference in the way you used to engage each other earlier in the relationship and how you do things today. For example, you text each other instructions these days yet you're all in the same house. Earlier in the relationship, you'd walk to where your spouse was and tell them what you needed them to do.

## Satisfaction

The longer your spouse spends on their devices, the more dissatisfied you feel in the relationship. This is an interesting one, because dissatisfaction isn't something that you can easily define or quantify. It's a feeling, one that eats away at your worthiness over time. When you're with someone who makes you feel like a stranger, knowingly or otherwise, you feel less inclined to be emotionally invested in the relationship.

## *Disconnection from Reality*

If you feel your spouse is disconnected from the reality of your lives, tell them about it. This is something that many people never realize. The longer your spouse spends on their devices, the easier it is for them to create a whole new reality that suits their needs. The problem with this escape is that it is virtual. At the end of the day, life goes on in the real world, and it passes your spouse by.

Use this moment to define your reality. How are things evolving in the relationship? How has your spouse's interaction with your kids changed? They may spend less time with the kids, and when they do spend time, their phone is likely close by, luring them in one notification at a time.

You've probably seen a lot of couples who set "couple goals" on social media, constantly posting and sharing things about their seemingly perfect lives. Sadly, most of these picture-perfect relationships don't last because away from the cameras, they are going through the same challenges we all are. If anything, they might even have deeper, bigger issues than you do.

As you engage your spouse on this matter, remind them of the strong connection you've always had, the foundation of your relationship. Then share that you feel the connection is getting shallower by the day, and you fear you might be losing them to whatever new excitement they found in their devices.

Chapter 2:

# The Effect on Your Relationship

*Wi-fi went down for five minutes, so I had to talk to my family. They seem like nice people.*

The damaging effect on tech in your life could be worse than you'd originally imagined. How did you get here? When you look at it this way, you're essentially thinking about how you and your spouse allowed tech into your lives. Of course, you'll be excused for pointing fingers at your better half, because their addiction to tech has you so frustrated. Yet, squaring it out with them is just a battle. The war isn't over yet.

Often, we limit our perception of the problems in our relationships to the battles we fight with our spouses. What most people don't realize is that other relationships exist outside or around our intimacy, and they equally feel the brunt of our squabbles. I'll give you one example—the effect of your spouse's tech addiction on your kids. You probably hadn't thought about that, right?

In the previous chapter, you may have had that *aha!* moment where you realized your relationship has a problem that must be addressed urgently. Your spouse's addiction to tech is draining the joy from your relationship, so much so that you feel like your spouse is cheating on you with their tech. In this chapter, we'll build on that, digging deeper into the detrimental effect that this addiction is having on your relationships.

Of course, we can't ignore the beauty of tech, especially in the world that we live in. I mean, look around you. Today tech giants like Meta (formerly Facebook) are working on the metaverse, a concept that's widely seen as the next giant leap in the evolution of the internet as we know it. We're also living in the age of artificial intelligence (AI); maybe you've tried your hand at ChatGPT already (if you haven't, spare a few minutes and have a go at it).

What I'm getting at is the fact that we cannot wish tech away. It is that necessary evil that makes life easier, streamlines processes, and offers many other benefits. At the same time, we cannot turn a blind eye to the dangers of such advancements. If anything, you're here because tech is ruining your relationship.

One of the biggest challenges that people who are addicted to tech go through is that they get so used to their devices that the devices almost feel like second nature to them. Therefore, such a person has a hard time realizing that they have a problem. You, on the other hand, whose needs have been neglected, who feel ignored, playing second fiddle to an inanimate object, feel the pain of isolation in your relationship.

That emptiness swallows you whole each time you're around your spouse, whether in the house or outside, when they pull out their device and get lost in it, seemingly having more fun than what they should be having with you. The emptiness can take a toll on you, making you question your worth. It can eat away at your esteem, and you can't just keep quiet and let that keep happening.

Things are not okay. This is not okay. Your spouse needs to understand how their addiction is affecting your relationship. This is the conversation you must have.

## Honey, We Have a Problem!

How do I call my spouse out on their tech addiction without sounding accusatory? This is one challenge everyone goes through in different forms in relationships. We all have moments when we really need to open up about something, but at the same time, we're worried, and rightly so, that talking about it might create a bigger mess than the issue we're trying to raise.

This feeling is not necessarily limited to our spouses. We've been in such situations with our friends, colleagues, and even parents. This is a typical conflict situation. Conflicts are a normal part of life. The challenge is how to resolve it amicably. Most people don't know how to do that, or even if they do, their spouses might not necessarily take it with the maturity that's required.

The fact is that tech is a problem in your relationship, and you're trying to arrest it before it creates a monster of its liking. So, how do you approach this?

The first thing is to realize that this is a "we" kind of problem, and because of that, the solution cannot come from a "you" perspective. Any solutions for the tech problem in your relationship will only be effective if you approach them as a team.

I need you to remember two things throughout this experience that will be crucial in not just helping you overcome the addiction problem, but in strengthening your relationship and in getting you back to building the life you'd envisioned with your spouse for many years:

1.  Your relationship is a choice you make every day.

2.  Relationships take work, a lot of work.

You're working with your spouse as a team. A team thrives in a cohesive environment. Cohesion, in your case, means care, effective communication, and empathy. Remember that despite this bump in your life, you're still committed to making the relationship work.

Since you're the spouse bringing this addiction discussion to the table, you have some control over how this will go. Its success depends on how you approach it. The first option is to raise complaints and basically attack your spouse, calling them out on their tech usage. Most people do that, and I can guarantee you that it never ends well. If anything, your spouse will most likely become defensive. They could even shut down emotionally to avoid escalating the issue, or simply to escape the criticism.

As you can see, the first option will only antagonize your spouse, and in the long run, you won't solve the problem. If anything, it could even drive another wedge between you two. In most cases, conflict exists in a relationship when either or both spouses do not understand their personal and personality differences, or overlook them altogether. Essentially, what you've done by attacking your spouse is to create a situation for emotional reaction, instead of an opportunity for rational conversation about the problem. At the end of the day, relationships should be about you and me against the problem, not each other.

The second option is much better than the first. It's an option that carries a lot of goodwill for one another and the relationship. It's an option that takes into consideration one another's feelings, thoughts, and more importantly, willingness to explore each other's perspectives on the conflict and come to a reasonable settlement. Instead of attacking your spouse, you take a moment and think about the conversation.

What outcome are you hoping for? Are you looking for an apology? Do you hope your spouse will understand your point of view? Do you wish to get closer to your spouse?

Let's face it. Their addiction to tech is but a symptom. So, if you're approaching this from the point of the addiction, you'll probably make little progress. On the other hand, if you approach it by looking at the underlying issue beyond the symptom, you have a better chance of making headway.

For example, your desired outcome could be spending more time with your spouse like you used to. You can initiate a conversation by reminiscing on the moments when you used to have more time for each other, then bring their attention to the fact that you don't seem to have that anymore.

You might not realize it, but you've already made this a "we" conversation, and you have a good chance that your spouse will be more interested in making things work. As you brainstorm possible reasons why you might not be spending quality time together, you can introduce their addiction to tech. You'd be surprised to learn that your spouse probably immerses themselves into their devices so much because they feel distant.

Relationships are complicated like that. At times we focus so much on what we're not getting out of them that we fail to realize that there's a chance our spouse's avoidant responses might be because we slacked off.

This conversation should inspire hope that your spouse will understand you, hope that you understand them, and more importantly, it may build anticipation that you are both committed to doing better for one another.

# Explore the Emotional Disconnect

You have your spouse's attention. You are both on the same page and agree that their tech use is pulling you two apart. This is the right moment to delve into the emotional aspect of the wedge you see in your relationship. You're trying to show your spouse that despite being physically in the same space, emotionally you are worlds apart, and that's not okay.

Emotional disconnect is never healthy for any relationship because that's how you gradually become estranged. It can get to the point where you'd rather be anywhere else but in the same space with your spouse. Let's not let it get to that.

An interesting thing about discussing the emotional disconnect in your relationship is that it's a subtle way of initiating a conversation about healthy boundaries. Sadly, boundaries tend to get a bad reputation everywhere. People generally assume that boundaries are a call for strictness, punishment, or some kind of restriction, but that isn't always true.

Boundaries essentially are about respect. Respect for one another, and more importantly, respect for the relationship. Healthy boundaries allow each of you to thrive within the relationship, such that you experience both individual and collective growth. By enforcing healthy boundaries, you're essentially creating a safe space where each spouse can grow without feeling like the other is trying to change them.

As your relationship evolves, the dynamics of your boundaries will keep adjusting because your life keeps changing. Maturity in the relationship means that despite the changes in your lives, emotionally, you should still be together.

So, how do you bring up the conversation about the emotional dissonance created by tech in your relationship? It's quite simple: Express your feelings.

We mentioned earlier that you have your spouse's attention. Building on that, tell them how you feel. Start the conversation with *"I feel"*. Here's an example:

*"I feel so frustrated when we're trying to spend some quality time together, but you get distracted by something on your phone. At times it makes me feel like you'd rather be somewhere else doing something else than spending time with me. It makes me feel unappreciated, and at times like I'm a bother to you."*

See how seamless that is?

Now, the fact that you have expressed your feelings doesn't necessarily mean that your spouse will respond kindly or with maturity, but you've done something huge. You've been honest about your feelings. The ball is now in their court, and their response, especially since you've been vulnerable with them about this, will show you how much they care about you and the relationship.

Being vulnerable with one another is something every relationship needs in order to thrive. Emotional distance gets in the way of your vulnerability. Instead of opening up, most people shut down because it feels like they're leaving themselves too exposed.

Emotional distance from your spouse is one of the most challenging issues to navigate, but you can close the gap. It calls for honest and open communication. You might even take a walk down memory lane to remind each other of what you used to have. This could be the fire that rekindles the lost spark in your relationship.

It's quite funny that one of the key reasons for emotional distance is usually a lack of communication. You can talk to one another often, but you barely communicate. Tech is especially notorious for fanning these flames.

The thing about devices is that losing yourself in them is so easy. You may start with something as simple as trying to beat that difficult level on Candy Crush or coming across an exciting meme channel. Before you know it, you're so hooked on your device that it's the first thing you reach out for when you wake up. At one time in the past, the first thing you reached out for was your spouse. Instead of pillow talk before you sleep, you're up late at night checking your social media timeline. This is how spouses lose the plot and the emotional distance grows.

As you move apart, you suddenly take each other's needs, desires, and feelings for granted. Perhaps you might have liked one or two of the memes your spouse shared earlier, but that doesn't mean that you're all in the way they are. This is what hurts. The misunderstanding sets in, where one spouse is living in their newfound tech world while the other is left wondering how they fit into that virtual world.

# Technology Robs You of Quality Time and Intimacy

How did we get here? Sure, you've addressed the emotional distance, but when or how did things start falling apart?

When your spouse is drawn to their tech beyond a healthy limit, you can easily point out the fact that they made their own choices. Unfortunately, there's actually a science to this. Where addiction exists, hormones are always at play. Allow me to explain this.

Devices and other tech products ruin your relationship by killing intimacy because they attack your relationship on a psychological level. While you might be noticing the physical distance and changes in your spouse's behavior, the biggest battle goes on in their minds.

The pleasure hormone (dopamine) and the bonding hormone (oxytocin) are always at play. Dopamine gets you excited. It's released when you're engaging in fun stuff, like eating chocolate, getting intimate with your spouse, and so on. Thanks to technology, you have excitement at your fingertips, so it's easier for the body to release dopamine. At times, all it takes is a glance at your Instagram reel and poof! You don't even need to make any effort. The brain finds it easy to get dopamine released with one glance at your phone, for example, instead of putting in the work for something like setting up an intimate night together, or just holding hands and going for a walk.

The brain releases oxytocin when you bond with your loved one through physical touch, shared experiences, and so on. As long as you are wholly and intentionally present in each other's space, oxytocin is being released.

As you can imagine, spending endless hours on your devices denies you the opportunity to bond. It gets worse because tech devices generally spam your brain with an information overload, especially if you spend a lot of time on social media.

It's clear, therefore, that even though you're communicating displeasure around the absence of physical appreciation, the emotional distance, and so on, the biggest battle your spouse needs to overcome is psychological. That is how tech has been ruining your lives, gradually robbing you of intimacy and quality time.

Apart from the psychological impact, tech also erodes your relationship by changing some behaviors. For example, before the tech addiction, you probably made a lot of calls to one another throughout the day. However, these days, you barely call each other. If anything, it's easier to just text instructions and hope they get the message and the context and, more importantly, that they address the instructions within the desired timelines.

To be honest, that's too many assumptions wrapped up in one message. You could have just called and talked about it, right?

This is also how misunderstandings creep into your relationship. For example, you wonder why they haven't texted you back. You're triggered by a word they used in their response. They send the wrong emoji, or even worse, they reply to your message without an emoji. You send an entire paragraph, but they respond with a curt sentence. It's quite infuriating. Yet, all this could have been avoided by calling. Instead, texting seemed the easier option.

You might not realize it, but what started as your spouse's addiction to their tech might soon rub off on you. You may be forced to find ways of coping, or just getting by, which might be quite unhealthy. Relationships take work, lots of it. You must be conscious and intentional about your actions and choices all the time.

## Effect on the Kids

The conversation about tech use and addiction is even more important if you have kids. Someone has to speak up for them because they certainly won't come to your spouse and complain that they aren't getting the attention they deserve. Your spouse may need to realize that you're not the only person struggling or suffering in this relationship because of their tech use. Your kids are losing touch with them, too.

The relationship between parents and children is a sacred one, and no child should ever be put in a position where they must compete for their parent's attention, especially not with a gadget or tech device the parent is addicted to. This is even more important in their earlier years.

For children under the age of 3, human interaction is one of the most important things for their growth and development. Anything that disrupts this interaction can have a profound influence on their lives and their relationships with people and the environment around them.

Tech interference in the parent-child relationship is particularly disturbing because children simply get accustomed to the fact that you're on your phone, and they won't question you about it. One of the worst things a child can go through is getting used to being ignored by a parent.

Tech is all around us, and while that is good news in some ways, we cannot pretend that all its consequences are beneficial. When it comes to the kids, we need to do the hard work. We need to put in the effort and have conversations with them, pay attention, and do everything possible to be intentionally present in their interactions with us. This is important because such interactions help children learn crucial skills which will come in handy for them when they start getting that immersive experience with tech later in life. It's up to the parents, therefore, to set the right foundation for healthy tech use. This means that you must set the right examples for your kids.

You could, for example, leave your phone in a separate room from where you're spending time with the kids. You can also turn off notifications during scheduled playtime with them. Even if you're not the addicted one, lots of suggestions could help you create that healthy relationship, and most of them require that you're intentional in your approach. Let's not rob our kids of the wholesome experiences they need to develop and grow into responsible adults.

Whichever option you choose, you have to be intentional about it. Remember that you're not just trying to help your spouse overcome this challenge, you're also trying to set the right examples for your kids to follow.

# Chapter 3:

# Leading by Example

*Little footprints in the sand usually follow larger ones, so watch where you step.*
—Frank Sonnenberg

Be the change you want to see in the relationship. This, perhaps, is the reality check that most spouses might not be ready to confront. Have you ever stopped to look in the mirror? Sure, your spouse's tech addiction has become a bother and you're working hard to help them overcome it, but do you ever stop to think about your own relationship with your devices?

Your challenges don't necessarily have to be about your devices, but you might have your own flaws with something else that your spouse might consider an addiction. Perhaps you're the kind of person who shares too much of their personal lives with their siblings. You can't help it. It's just the way you were brought up.

I mean, who could fault you? You've shared everything in your life with your sister or brother since you were kids, and keeping something from them seems awkward. You feel there's nothing to hide about your relationship, and that's why they are the first person who comes to mind whenever something significant is happening in your life.

No one is perfect. Because your spouse's tech addiction is the reason you picked this book, you may overlook the fact that you might similarly have your own flaws that need to be addressed. When couples are going through a difficult time in their relationships, the aggrieved spouse naturally sheds light on the problem they're trying to address, while ignoring their own flaws. It's just human nature.

We are wired for self-preservation, and that's one of the obstacles that you must work through if you are to help your spouse overcome their tech addiction. Look in the mirror. A moment of introspection can

29

give you better insight into the right way to approach this addiction issue with your spouse.

What if, for example, the tables were turned and your spouse raised concerns about your own flaws? How would you want them to address it? You'd probably want them to confront your flaws in a peaceful, loving manner. You'd want them to show that despite their attempts at helping you overcome this problem, they still care for you and are committed to walking the journey with you. You'd need assurance that they would be there for you through the recovery process, hold your hand when things are getting harder, and help you pick up the pieces if there's ever a need to do so.

With this insight, how do you set the right examples? Don't just tell your spouse what to do, show them the right way to come back to you. If you have kids, this is just as important for them as it is for you and your spouse. Children learn best by watching what the adults around them do, rather than what they say.

Most of the time, couples assume that their relationships are only about the two of them. They assume that the decisions they make can only affect them. The unfortunate truth is that what happens in your relationship could affect more than just the two of you—not just your kids, but anyone else who's living with you, including your nannies, parents, or siblings.

Therefore, be aware of the fact that you are not just setting an example for your spouse on the best way to use tech, you're also the beacon of hope for everyone around you. Your words, choices, and actions are being noticed. If you speak harshly to your spouse about their tech addiction, everyone else picks up on that. The respect or disrespect you choose when handling this will be mirrored by everyone in your household.

So, the question you must ask yourself is whether you're setting a good or a bad example for your household.

Genuine love—that's the thing that should come to mind when you reflect on this experience some years down the line. If anyone ever asks you how your relationship survived your spouse's tech addiction, that's the simplest answer you could give them.

The goal here isn't just overcoming your spouse's tech addiction or assessing your own tech habits or any other flaws you might have, but to come up with a lasting solution. You're not just solving an immediate problem, you're setting the foundation for future success. We cannot escape tech, so we must learn how to be productive in the relationship and in our lives with technology. This is a struggle that you might be fighting at home, but maybe you don't realize that your spouse might also be struggling with this beyond your household. You have to step in and be proactive because this could cost them their jobs and their relationship, and when those two are gone, they're on a slippery slope that could even cost them their lives.

The desired outcome is to live and lead a successful and fulfilling life. It's to come up with effective strategies that can help you both navigate life and the challenges of your relationship in a healthy manner. Remember that these are the skills you'll also be sharing with your kids, so getting this right is also in their best interest.

## Assessing Your Tech Habits

How would you rate your tech use in the relationship? Would you consider it harmful or not? How do you think your own tech use affects your relationship?

A proper assessment of your tech use can be a difficult, yet revealing, experience. You should do one so that you know what your role in the tech dilemma is. It's important for your spouse to know that you've considered your role when you confront them about their tech use.

Confronting someone about something they are doing wrong isn't an easy task because it feels like an accusation. As a result, they could get defensive, and the entire conversation might not be productive at all. On the other hand, if you approach your spouse having explored and tried to understand your own flaws, you may find the issue easier to address because you can show them that you are in the same boat.

At the end of the day, a relationship works because you both realize that you are not perfect. You both understand that you appreciate and care for each other despite your imperfections, and you are both committed to doing and becoming better.

## Your Own Tech Use

Your phone is the most common tech culprit in the house, so start with that. How would you describe your screen time?

Take a few days to map your screen time. The good news is that lots of apps can help you with that. Install one of them from your app store, then monitor your device use patterns over a given period of time, say a week or two. Your usage statistics will tell you much more about your phone use than you've ever imagined.

For example, you'll see which apps or websites you visit frequently and how long you spend on them. Apart from that, you'll also notice how soon you pick up your phone after you wake up. For most people, it's the first thing they reach out for as soon as they are up. While it makes sense in that you want to check if you missed any calls, messages, alarms, or important notifications, it's not necessarily a good habit.

Do you have phone-free times, or are you the kind of person who must always have their phone in the room, even when they don't need it? How do you feel when you leave your phone in another room? Do you frequently pop in to check if you missed something, or do you just get on with your schedule and come back to your phone if it rings?

What about your free time? How does your phone fit into your free time? Is your phone your engagement activity when you're free, or can you sit down and watch something, read a book, or step outside without worrying about leaving your phone behind?

Now, these are questions that we should all learn to ask ourselves because they reveal so much about our own usage behavior. They also give us insight into the kind of life or struggles that your spouse might be going through, hence their addiction. Remember, as we mentioned earlier, the conversations you're meant to have with your spouse about their tech use should be inspired by genuine love. You care for your spouse, and your relationship, that's why you're taking these steps.

Addiction is a word we throw around carelessly, especially when our needs are not being met and we think we can easily identify the reasons why. Occasionally, we all feel like we're addicted to our devices. We have that one time when we can't seem to put our phone down. A massive scandal could have blown up on the social media site X and we just can't afford to not know what's happening. After all, everyone's talking about it. It's all over the news, so it's only natural that we'd want to get in on the know.

But whether your compulsion is out of addiction or a one-time thing is another question altogether, hence the need to assess and understand your tech use behavior. The fact is that even though we live in a time when most people spend too much time online and on our devices, not many people are actually addicted to a point where they feel like their lives depend on their devices. If anything, addiction exists on a spectrum, so someone who's struggling with a tech addiction could be anywhere from mildly to severely affected.

As you look into your tech behavior, consider the possibility that you might have as bad a habit as your spouse does, and you may not realize it because your spouse hasn't called you out on it yet.

## Compulsive Use

Sure, you don't bury your face in your phone like your spouse does, but you cannot go anywhere without it. You feel that leaving your phone behind means being unreachable. As long as your phone is on you all the time, you can easily create those random moments when you just can't let it go. For example, you spend more time in the toilet with your phone than without it. It's quite weird how uncomfortable the toilet seat is, yet it somehow always feels so cozy when you're in there with your phone.

A compulsive user is someone who feels like they need to do something all the time, even when they know they have no reason to do it and nothing bad would happen if they didn't do it. Does this feel like something you can relate to?

The problem with compulsive tech use is that it overrides your rational thought patterns. For example, your notification tone or light comes on while you're driving, and you instantly reach for the phone to see what it's about. You have no reason to do so, and ignoring your phone until the next stop seems a better option, but you opt against that, and instantly reach for the device.

## Modeling Healthy Tech Use Through Self-Regulation

Self-regulation is one of the best ways to set a good example, not just for your spouse but also for your kids. Self-regulation implies that you know your limits. It's also a crucial aspect of setting healthy boundaries for the use of tech in your household, a concept we'll explore further in the next chapter. You cannot create healthy tech use behavior without the ability to self-regulate. You must first know your limits and from there, come up with mutually acceptable ways of enforcing them.

Building on the concept of setting the right examples, you must create the right model for your spouse and everyone else in your household to follow. You can't call your spouse out on their tech use while you're struggling equally with the same thing or something else. While kids generally learn best by observing the adults around them, adults can also do the same.

For example, if you make a habit of leaving your phone out of the bedroom, your spouse might pick up on that and give it a try. Trying to hold people to standards that you're unable to meet yourself is unfair.

Here are some screen habits that you could consider implementing to set the right example for your household:

- Keep your phone away when having conversations with friends or family. If your phone is in the vicinity, leave it be. Don't look at it each time the screen lights up. If you have to have it nearby, put it on silent mode.

- Don't use your phone as an escape from boredom.

- Don't let your phone be the first thing you touch when you wake up.

- Unplug unnecessary devices at night, especially when you go to sleep. That could include anything from your phone to the television.

If you'd rather not see these habits in your spouse, you must set the right example. When you're with your spouse, leave your phone on mute and on the charging dock. Beyond that, another important tactic you'll need to learn is the concept of time.

Set time limits on your tech use. This might not necessarily be relevant to your spouse, but it makes a big difference for your kids. Teach your kids about time management, and the opportunity cost of time lost doing something that doesn't add value to their lives as opposed to something productive. Remind them that nothing is wrong with using their devices, they just need to be mindful of why and when they use them.

A simple approach to this is to spend time with your child, away from their devices and yours. Take them out into the yard and spend 10 minutes with them. Use this time to ask questions or have them ask you questions. Enjoy the environment, help them refine their sensory skills. You're creating a positive influence in their lives, which no amount of tech will ever do for them.

Finally, and this works for both your spouse and the kids, learn to be mindful of your body, especially when you've been using gadgets for a while. We hardly pay attention to the physical impact of tech on our bodies. You might feel exhausted, straining, or in some pain but brush it off as the effect of having a difficult day at work. You might not realize this, but spending too much time on your devices can be detrimental to your health.

Here are some things you should be mindful about:

- your posture when using your devices

- your breathing patterns

- whether your neck hurts when you're using your devices, probably from craning over.

While these do look like common signs of a long day at work, they have also been linked to excessive use of tech. The worst thing about it is that even though your spouse might be conscious about this, your kids might not be. Everyone needs to know when they've had too much of their gadgets and they need to put them down and do something else.

Technology isn't going anywhere. In fact, it's only getting better and more integrated into our lives. The most important thing is for you to learn how to unplug from it all and set clear, healthy guidelines for your household. Be the champion for the change you want to see in your relationship.

## Stronger Through Mutual Efforts

Given what you've discovered about your tech use habits, what should you do to improve your relationship? This is about the mutual effort you'll invest in the relationship with your spouse, because if you're going to win this battle, you have to do it together.

Most self-aware people have a love-hate relationship with tech. The fact is that we cannot do without it, so we have to find a way to coexist peacefully with it. The distraction, fixation on social media, scrolling through your phone all day, playing games, taking pictures everywhere you go—we are all guilty of that. However, all these things do is distract you from the real thing you should be doing, living your life.

Having learned how to self-regulate, here are some simple tips you can implement with your spouse. Remember, this is not necessarily about getting your spouse to address their addiction but showing them that there's a better way to do things. By setting the right examples, you make it easier for your spouse to reflect on their behavior and choose to confront their demons. If things don't work out, let it not be for lack of trying. You can only do so much to guide an adult. Beyond that, they must make their own choices and take responsibility for them.

## Usage Limits

This comes off our discussion about assessing your screen time. Once you're aware of your excessive usage, do something about it. If your phone has the function, set app usage limits. You could also download an app to assist with that. The same concept applies to other things like video games or television. Figure out an appropriate amount of time that you'd be comfortable using the device without interfering with your lives, and work with that.

## Push Notifications

You can miss out on the gossip by a few minutes or hours. Most of the notifications on your phone don't necessarily require your attention. Turn them off, and similarly, turn off the notification sounds. The rings and beeps are just as distracting as your screen lighting up. This is, perhaps, one of the most proactive steps you can take to win back your time and attention from your devices.

## A Fresh Start

Rethink your approach to a new day. How do you start the day? If, like most people, the first thing you do is to check your phone when you wake up, change that. Put your phone on airplane mode when you go to sleep. Put your phone away from your bedside, so you can't physically stretch and reach for it when you wake up.

So what do you do when you wake up, now that your phone has been isolated from your mornings? Well, get up and move around. Jump into the kitchen and make breakfast, or whatever you enjoy in the morning. Go wake up the kids and play with them a bit. Do anything but think of, or touch, your phone. You're essentially creating a tech-free morning routine. Once you're done with the routine, freshen up and turn on your phone.

Here's the interesting thing—you can reach out to anyone who tried to get in touch with you but couldn't find you. Call them back. You'll notice that the world didn't stop because you were unreachable for a few hours.

## Be Intentional

Do something because you want to do it, and you know why it's important to you. When you take a break from tech, be intentional about it. This builds on the previous point. You turned your phone off because you wanted to create a tech-free morning routine, then you turned your phone back on when you were ready.

Tech-free is not just about your morning. You could take a few tech days off. You could decide to stay off tech on weekends, take a month, or choose any other schedule that works for you. You could also leave your phone behind when you step out for a walk or to run errands. The point here is that you need to learn how to detach your phone from your life. It's not a shadow that follows you everywhere you go.

## Mindful Tech Use

Once you're intentional about your usage, becoming mindful about what you do with your devices or how you use them is much easier. For example, pay attention to people's tech behavior in a restaurant. Phones come out as soon as the food gets placed on the table. They take photos and post them online. Nothing is really wrong with that, as long as they're not infringing on anyone's rights.

However, do you really have to do it?

How many food photos can you take until it becomes too much? If you're a food blogger or earn a living from taking such photos, then by all means, go on and earn your keep. On the other hand, if you're doing it just for fun and memories, you don't have to snap everything. Your attention gets drawn from savoring your meal to taking the most picturesque photos of it. Go ahead and enjoy your meal without the photos!

The beauty of tech is that it empowers you to learn. Why don't you leverage this to learn more about yourself? You can learn from watching what others do—for example, the people taking food photos in a restaurant—and decide what's healthy for your relationship and what needs to go. Once you can use yourself as the subject, you become aware of useful information about your own tech use. With this insight, you can make better decisions for your relationship and the technology around you.

# Chapter 4:

# Navigating Technology

# Boundaries

*We feel used and mistreated when we fail to set boundaries and hold people accountable. This is why we sometimes attack who they are, which is far more hurtful than addressing a behavior or a choice.* —Brené Brown

Can you remember a time when communication in your relationship was open, honest, and just felt right? Your conversations were always calm and full of warmth, and more importantly, you looked forward to them. Those were good days. These days, not so much, right?

Healthy communication is the glue that binds relationships together. Now that your spouse's tech addiction is threatening your relationship, addressing it is one of the strategies that can help you fight your way back to the love you once had for one another.

The fact is that tech will always be around you. Technology is part and parcel of the modern lifestyle, so you have to make peace with that. At the same time, however, you're also smart enough to realize that you can use tech in better ways and make sure that it does not cause more harm than good.

Having open, healthy communication with your spouse is possible despite the prevalence of tech around you. You can reignite that connection you used to have with your spouse without being oblivious to the importance of tech in your lives. To achieve this, you must both be intentional in your approach. This is where healthy boundaries come in.

Like we mentioned earlier, boundaries don't always have to be about restrictions. If you look at boundaries from a restrictive perspective, you'll never be able to see any good coming from them. On the other hand, if you see boundaries as a means of expressing your concerns, needs, and expectations to your spouse, you can use them to rebuild trust in your relationship.

## *Setting Boundaries*

How do you go about setting boundaries? Well, first, you must be aware of the pertinent problem in the relationship. In this case, it's your spouse's addiction to their devices. Take a moment and reflect on how the addiction is affecting your relationship. How does the addiction interfere with getting your needs met? What has changed in your relationship? This moment of reflection helps you understand why the boundaries are necessary. This clarity will be crucial in having the difficult conversation with your spouse.

Next, talk to your spouse about it. Now, in most cases, this is the difficult part. You need your spouse to take this conversation seriously, so you have to be both assertive and kind. You don't want to set a tone that makes them want to fight back. Instead, try to express your needs and feelings in a respectful manner, even though you're feeling hurt and distant. Remember that this is not meant to invalidate your feelings, but to set the right environment for healthy boundaries that you can both commit to.

Periodically follow up with your spouse to ensure the boundaries are working for you and your relationship. Remember that this is supposed to be mutually beneficial, and not a one-sided experience. For example, you might have to take drastic measures, like creating a watershed period where you turn off certain devices so you can try to reconnect with each other. It might be a difficult step, but at times difficult steps are necessary, especially where your well-being and mental health in the relationship are concerned.

## Your Spouse Isn't On Board Yet... What Next?

Now that you're on the subject of boundaries, you face the real possibility that your spouse might not be willing to hear you out. Granted, this conversation would be easy if they heard your point of view and made a commitment to doing better, but unfortunately, we don't always get everything we want in life. That's probably one of the realest lessons you learn as an adult.

So, you're in a position where you've laid your concerns bare to your spouse, but they either aren't listening or they are having a difficult time accepting the points you're trying to put across. At this point, it's quite evident that you need to enforce boundaries, otherwise, your spouse will continue to walk all over you on this.

I must point out that even though you're at a point where enforcing boundaries is the way to go, you must not appear as though you're steamrolling over your spouse. Getting them on board might not be the easiest thing to do at this point, but you can still try to help them see your perspective while also making an effort to consider theirs. The end goal here is to awaken their intuition or instinct to the reality that you are not in a good place as a couple, and you both need to do something about it.

For a spouse who's not on board, you can expect accusations, annoyance, embarrassment, or some kind of tension when you try to hunker down on this conversation. The reason for this is that tech use, especially when your spouse is constantly on their phone, is a gray area in many intimate relationships. It comes down to the uncomfortable question: What is ours, what is mine, and what is yours?

Let's take it a notch higher and put yourself in your spouse's shoes. What would be your reaction, for example, if they asked to look at your phone or the browsing history on your laptop?

Even though you might not have anything to hide, a sense of uneasiness sets in when someone poses such questions to you. That's what your spouse might be going through right now, hence their defensiveness. Often, probing into your spouse's tech use raises an issue of trust, and where trust is questioned, things can go south so fast. How do you arrest this situation?

Well, every cloud truly does have a silver lining. Your relationship is facing a crisis right now. However, this is also an opportunity that you can both seize and turn things around. The hurt and confusion you're experiencing right now could easily bring you closer to one another, depending on how you approach these conversations.

The opportunity presented in your relationship right now is one where you have a deep and honest conversation. Ignoring it, as your spouse may do, will be at your own peril. This is a moment of growth, and as a couple, you should make the most of it. Remember, intimacy dies when you stop having difficult conversations in your relationship. You're probably at that point, but all is not lost yet.

Here are some ideas you can explore with your spouse, and hopefully, this could get them thinking about their role in this impasse.

- Help me understand how we can work together and set healthy boundaries around the use of tech in our relationship, because I feel what we have right now is affecting our relationship negatively.

- I feel we've gotten carried away and aren't investing as much effort and time in our relationship as we used to do earlier. How can we get back on track?

- I feel you're spending more time on your devices, so much that even when we're together in the same room, you're so distant. I feel I'm losing you to your devices, and that's not okay. How can we help each other through this?

- I'm not refuting the value of tech in our lives, and I respect your space. However, I feel we need to be more intentional in the way we use tech in this house, especially when we should be spending quality time together. How can we hold each other accountable for this?

From the statements above, you've set the tone for a difficult, yet important, conversation. If your spouse wasn't on board, this should stop them in their tracks. You've added valuable context to the conversation, and this should be enough to get them thinking about the depths of this conversation.

At this point, you will both share insight on the questions and statements above and, hopefully, your spouse will realize the magnitude of the problem.

So, where are we heading with this?

Well, ultimately, you'll need to set some guidelines to help your relationship bounce back to healthy face-to-face communication. As far as the use of tech is concerned, you can explore many rules. Here are some suggestions that have worked for many thriving couples, and which I believe could be a good place for you to start:

- Keep devices away from the dinner table. If possible, leave them outside the room altogether.

- Don't use your phones when you're eating at a restaurant. You could even go a notch higher and leave them in the car.

- If you're in the same space, say at home, don't text or call one another on the phone. This is actually a common problem in many relationships these days. If you need to say something, walk to where your spouse is and tell them what you want to say.

- Unless it's urgent, personal or important issues should be discussed in person, not over the phone. This way you get not just the message, but also the appropriate context, feelings, emotions, and other sentiments around it.

As you can see from the above, you must be intentional in your approach if you wish to have a healthy conversation with your spouse about their tech addiction. Finding a solution comes down to creating an environment that works for both of you in equal measure, where neither feels like they're compromising too much for the other.

Remember, this isn't about fighting each other, but about the two of you fighting against the problem.

# Tips for Setting Healthy Tech Use Boundaries in Your Relationship

Clearly at this point in the relationship, neither of you is getting all your needs met. Your spouse's tech addiction is frustrating. The need for healthy tech boundaries in your relationship is a matter of urgency. You should know that even though you're working toward setting boundaries, the way you approach this could make a big difference in whether the boundaries work for your relationship or not. Boundaries should be about more than just setting guidelines on what works or how to do things, but also about respect and appreciating one another.

If you're going to set healthy boundaries that work for your relationship, you must be the best role model. It's impossible to honestly champion something you don't believe in or subscribe to. Set the right example for your spouse to emulate. Remember that if you have kids, the examples you are setting with your spouse will go a long way in determining what the kids learn from you about tech use in their relationships. For example, asking your spouse to keep their phone away from the dinner table would be futile if yours keeps buzzing just a glance away.

## *Why Boundaries Help*

Despite the fact that you're taking this approach to help your spouse overcome their addiction, tech boundaries also go a long way in protecting your family. Relationships, whether with your spouse, your kids, or your extended family, are built around genuine connections. That is why you miss each other when you're not around. You cannot have that connection with someone who's frequently distracted with their devices. You know this because you probably had a time when you had a strong connection with your spouse, but since they started spending more time on their devices than with you, you've become strangers living under the same roof.

Healthy boundaries, therefore, go a long way in protecting the sanctity of the close bonds that hold your family together. They're also about creating a safe and healthy environment at home. Spending quality time with your spouse and your family is good for your physical and mental health, so in the long run, you're going to achieve so much more than just helping your spouse overcome their tech addiction. You're fighting a battle to save and protect your family.

Another reason why you need to set boundaries is that they are a refresher course on how to work together. Take a moment and think about it. Before your spouse's tech addiction started, you had lots of things you used to do together that you don't do anymore. This isn't even about going shopping or doing other shared activities together, but something as fundamental as planning. You'd sit down and make plans together, iron out the differences, discuss the compromises, and come up with a steady set of steps that worked for the greater good of your household. You don't do that anymore.

When you sit down to discuss tech boundaries, you're essentially asking your spouse to come back to the drawing board with you. As a household, you're tracing your steps back to the time when you'd explore the pros and cons of every option together. The goal here is also to show your spouse that you are committed to this process, and you value their input.

One of the main reasons why you have to get back to planning together is that creating boundaries means you must also discuss consequences for breaching the agreement. Boundaries become effective when clear consequences are established, and this is how you hold one another accountable. The repercussions for breaching the boundaries must be enforced unapologetically if this process is to work.

The concept of consequences by itself, underscores the importance of working together to create healthy boundaries. Put yourself in your spouse's shoes for a moment. How would you feel if you came home one day and your significant other handed you a list of do's and don'ts, and consequences for going against the contents of that list? You'd feel like they were trying to control you, make your life harder, or even impose unrealistic sanctions on the relationship.

On the other hand, if they approached this through an open and honest discussion, mentioning their worries and fears over your addiction and what it's done to the relationship, you'd think differently about it. They'd welcome you to discuss possible solutions, and you'd also share suggestions that would work for the relationship. That's how you build healthy and sustainable boundaries. The goal is not to alienate your spouse, but to remind them that they are a part of the solution.

Finally, even though it seems like an insurmountable task at the moment, do not be afraid. You can work together to create the healthy boundaries that will work for your relationship. You just have to be brave, and be kind to one another while at it.

# Negotiating Mutually Acceptable Guidelines for Device Usage

I can sum up this section in one phrase—spouseship!

Our previous discussion about the value of healthy boundaries makes evident that the only way you can make this a success is if you work together. You're not imposing sanctions on your spouse to put their devices away, but helping them understand why they need to do so. When you work together, understanding each other's point of view gets easier, and in the long run, you can rebuild the trust you had in each other.

Every relationship is a spouseship. It's your daily reminder that you are both working for the greater good of the relationship. It's a reminder that each of your interests is valid.

Remember that working together also means that you'll respect your spouse's desire to indulge in their tech from time to time. Tech is all around us, so wishing it away is impractical. Perhaps your spouse's use of tech is a necessary part of their job. However, working together also means that they must respect your desire to have them be more present in the relationship than they are right now. This is a give-and-take kind of situation, so the guidelines you work on must be mutually acceptable.

Let's explore some useful suggestions that could help you create mutually beneficial guidelines for tech use in your relationship.

## Tech-Free Time

This is one of the biggest steps that will be a win for your relationship. Designate specific times when you both detach from your tech and enjoy quality time with one another. You'd be surprised at the list of things you can do together without interference from tech. Mealtimes, game nights with the family, or a walk in the park.

You must be intentional for these decisions to work. For example, some families keep devices away a short while before and after mealtimes. This makes family bonding easier even before they share a meal. When you do that, you're not just bonding over the meal, but you're fostering deeper connections beyond that.

## Avoid Comparisons

This is your spouse. This is your relationship. This is your family. Your commitment is to make things work with these three pillars in your life. Sure, you might know a few couples who do things differently and it works for them, but that's their story.

Despite what your friends might tell you, no two households will ever be alike. What works in their relationships works because they have different goals and dreams than you do. If you try to implement the same approach in your household, you stand a good chance of failing because you know nothing of their motivations.

At the end of the day, every decision you make with your spouse should be against the backdrop of the core values you share. That is the foundation on which your relationship is built.

# Teachable Moments

We get lots of learning opportunities in life that we never take advantage of. This is one such moment for you, your spouse, and your family. As you work together on creating healthy boundaries, make use of this opportunity to explore and learn more together as a household about the pros and cons of adverse tech use.

Lots of documentaries and books that are great for the family could inspire a cultural shift in the way technology is used in your household. Even though all we think of is the immediate needs being satisfied by the use of tech, we can learn a lot about the impact of unhealthy tech use on the brain, relationships, and mental health. Such valuable information will go a long way in your household.

By setting mutually acceptable guidelines for your household, you're making big steps in the right direction. While tech is great for entertainment, connecting with loved ones over long distances, and for educational purposes, it can only serve these roles when used in the right manner. Setting clear guidelines is one way of ensuring that the use of tech does not distract your household from the positive functions we've mentioned.

Ultimately, your role as adults in the household is to ensure that you create an environment or a culture where screens and other gadgets do not become the sole source of entertainment, learning, or connecting with each other. The guidelines you set don't always have to be punitive or restrictive. Healthy guidelines allow you to indulge in your tech without disrupting the natural dynamics of your relationship. Healthy boundaries put technology in its rightful place.

Finally, even as you work on navigating the boundaries for healthy communication and use of tech in your relationship, it's important not to lose sight of the core issues in the relationship. This is as much about expressing your feelings and thoughts, and getting them heard, as it is about helping your spouse overcome their tech addiction.

At the end of the day, the point of setting boundaries is to help you:

- create a healthy environment where you can both listen to each other's pain points and views on the tech and communication issues without feeling or being disrespected.

- learn how to stand up for what you believe in.

- establish boundaries that help you prevent resentment and conflicts in the future, especially around the use of tech and the role it plays in your lives.

- establish reasonable consequences for breaching the boundaries, which inspires mutual self-respect in the relationship.

Ideally, the concept of healthy boundaries in the relationship is to help you and your spouse establish clear guidelines for what is acceptable and what is not. This, ultimately, is also about your well-being. When used appropriately, healthy boundaries can help you feel safe, and respected in the relationship. This is crucial in building trust, particularly in the way you communicate with one another.

# Chapter 5:

# Finding Balance in the Digital

# World

*In all aspects of our lives balance is key. Doing one thing too much can cause upset, like the old saying goes, everything in moderation is the secret!* —Catherine Pulsifer

The healthy balance of tech and quality time that once held your relationship together is long gone. Your relationship has since been robbed of the well-being and safety that were once your pillars of strength. But don't worry. They're not gone forever. Now is the time to bring them back.

The core of this chapter is to remind you that it's never too late to do the work. Even though your spouse is grossly addicted to their devices, all hope is not lost. You can build on the progress you made in creating healthy boundaries, and work on them to find a good balance that allows you to enjoy each other's company without the incessant interference of technology casting a gloomy cloud over your relationship.

One thing people don't realize about tech is the ease with which it bombards you with information. You're constantly hooked on screens and gadgets that feed you stories, pictures, social media posts, memes, emails, and so much more. You want to be the first one to know when something happens, when the biggest sale is happening, when your favorite movie is screening, and so on. Even though this information might be useful at times, the constant flow can overwhelm your brain.

From social media to news outlets and shopping updates, all the notifications on your devices create an insatiable desire to remain connected to the world around you, albeit digitally. Unfortunately, the longer you revel in the digital connection, the more you disconnect from the real world around you. This includes the people you love, the activities you enjoy, and so on. That's how you become a shell of yourself, because you're so engrossed in what's happening in the world on your palms that you forget about the world that exists around you.

Given the prominence of tech in our lives, the line between the digital world and the real world is very thin. For the sake of your relationship, you must strike a healthy balance between the two.

Picture this scenario:

A quiet evening, a cozy room, and the soft glow of candlelight replacing the harsh illumination of screens and soundtracks in your headsets. You're probably cuddled up with your spouse on the sofa, reading a book, or listening to some soft music.

This doesn't necessarily have to be a movie scene. This is the life you are meant to have with your spouse. If anything, you've had this before. You just lost your way some time ago, but you can work your way back to each other. These blissful moments are your reminder that in a world that's harsh and unforgiving, you found your forever person and pledged your love to one another. You promised to care and protect one another and to build a nurturing environment within which your love would flourish.

You can do a lot to find your way back to each other, to establish that healthy balance you seek. For this chapter, however, we'll focus on three core aspects that cut across most relationships: shared activities, quality tech-free time, and the power of reconnecting with one another. These three are important because they underpin every relationship you'd wish to rebuild. Whether the relationship is with your spouse, your kids, or your parents, they will always be the foundation of finding your way back to the ones you love.

# Shared Activity Without Technology

Let's take technology out of the equation for a moment. Use this opportunity to reconnect with your spouse. Having explored the value of setting boundaries around the use of tech in your relationship, you are both now willing to take steps toward rebuilding a stronger, more loving relationship. This is the beginning of your journey to rediscovering your commitment to one another.

Go offline for a while. This bold step could make a big difference in your rediscovery journey by helping you dive back into the kind of activities you both shared and enjoyed before tech disrupted the peace and harmony in your relationship. You're disconnecting from the internet and using the new-found time to rediscover your passion for hobbies and other activities you once loved to do together.

For clarity, this section is purely about an activity that does not involve any tech at all. I do understand that you might have some shared activities that could involve tech. We will explore those activities in the last section. Consider this section your cold turkey move.

So, what can you do with your spouse that involves no tech at all? This is an easy one—cook something.

It's funny how culinary delights can rekindle your romantic connection. We all have to eat, so meal creation is a sure winner. This works best for couples who love to cook, so if that isn't your thing, don't worry. You still can learn a thing or two that you can implement in a shared activity you both enjoyed before tech threatened your relationship.

Cooking a meal is more than just transforming food from ingredients to a ready meal on the table. There's the preparation, the delicate dance with ingredients, getting the heat just right, the spices, and finally, cleaning up the mess y'all made. While some people might feel this is an arduous task, for a couple that's passionate about the finer details, dinnertime can be the perfect bonding session, right there in your kitchen.

The beauty of cooking together is that it mirrors your relationship. No relationship is perfect. For it to work, you must learn how to blend the right ingredients together from time to time. You must know when to turn up the heat, or when to turn it down. You must know when to preheat the oven. You must know when to bring out the air fryer, or when to use the microwave.

Cooking together means working together, sharing ideas and instructions, taking turns to stir the pot, and so on. It's a delicate balance that culminates in an amazing meal. When it's all said and done, you have to wash the dishes and leave the kitchen sparkling clean. The act of cleaning is a subtle reminder that even in your relationship, the two of you are the only ones who can clean up your mess. Don't expect someone else to pick up the pieces for you.

No one knows the nooks and crannies of your relationship better than you do, so no one can clean up your mess better than you can. Working together in the kitchen doesn't just foster a sense of collaboration, but it also highlights the shared responsibility that each of you has in making sure you have a proper meal on the table.

In the time that your relationship was under the spell of *technoference*, your kitchen might have turned into a solo experience. The bliss of shared responsibility might have disappeared, but the two of you can bring it back. What you have right now is a situation where each spouse brings their creativity, skills, and ideas to the table.

One thing I love about cooking together with my spouse is the way it becomes a tangible way to care for, love, and express dedication to one another. Every step in the cooking process echoes the rhythm of a relationship that doesn't just work but is seamlessly harmonious.

How do you choose the right recipe? First, explore options together, because at the end of the day, you want this meal to be something that you'll both enjoy. Sounds familiar? The recipe selection process is symbolic because it's a reminder of how you made decisions earlier in the relationship. Choosing a meal is about communication and compromise. It's about teamwork, making the process the perfect microcosm of your relationship—a space where you learn to navigate differences and celebrate shared goals.

In retrospect, every step along the way from choosing the ingredients and spices to having the meal on the table is a parallel reflection of the journey your relationship has been through. You'll make adjustments along the way, you'll encounter challenges at each turn, but in the long run, you find joy in the final outcome because of the shared effort.

So what if you're not as passionate about cooking as your spouse is? Well, make an effort. Go out of your comfort zone and follow them into the kitchen. Make them laugh, tell some jokes, ask them how you can help. Your spouse is well aware of the fact that cooking isn't something you fancy, but the fact that you're expressing interest and your willingness to assist is a game changer.

You could help by simply stirring the pot or throwing ingredients into the blender. It might not be much, but it's an honest day's work, and that means a lot to your spouse.

Shared culinary moments like these enhance your emotional connection, bringing you closer. They are also reminders of what you might have lost, and why this was a timely save, a moment that probably changed your lives. Cooking together transcends the physical preparation of your meal. It is one of the most effective shared activities that have been proven over the years to nourish the soul.

Preparing a meal fosters a deep sense of mutual support and interdependence. Your kitchen becomes a safe space where vulnerabilities can be shared, and trust is reinforced through the act of creating and providing for one another.

# Quality Time

Shared activities are awesome, as we've outlined in the previous section. However, if you're looking for balance in the digital world, you must go beyond that. This section will explore the importance of tech-free time to the relationship. Keep in mind, though, that this time doesn't always have to involve a shared activity. Your spouse's tech-free time doesn't have to be hinged on your presence. Your spouse needs to see the value of it, especially when you're not around to nudge them into the tech-free zone.

Let's face it, our spouses can be babies at times, so this approach is about maturity, helping them realize that they need to grow up and take accountability for their role and actions in the relationship. If your spouse is only taking steps to do better when you're around, you're probably not making any progress. This is because they are not necessarily doing the right thing for the greater good of the relationship, but for you. In such a case, the progress you're making is but a smokescreen, and behind the scenes, your spouse might not be as committed to the process as you are. This is unsustainable, and at some point, the house of cards will cave in.

While your attention is on finding better ways to reconnect with your spouse, it's equally important to make sure that your solutions are not limited to tech. Tech-free time is essential in every relationship because it allows you to set the rest of the world aside and focus on each other. Start by talking to your spouse about an ideal time in their schedule when they feel they could comfortably detach from the digital world. This is a bold step because you're essentially asking your spouse to be a part of the solution, not ostracizing them for their role in creating the problem.

Creating such times in your schedule is important because they give you the space to talk about your day, your struggles, and any other issue that you might be going through as a couple. During this time you can share as much of the challenges together as you can share the joys. You can find ways to support each other in whatever you're working on.

Here are some simple strategies that you can explore together.

## Personal Quality Time

Create a special time for your relationship. This should be a dedicated space, not to be interrupted by your kids, work, or anything else. It's all about you and your relationship. Life is hard, especially when you think of the responsibilities, bills, and plans you have for the future. Many couples lose themselves in the grind, to a point where they become estranged yet they live under the same roof and share the same bed. Try the following ideas with your spouse.

## Date Night

Schedule a specific day and time for couple activities or just date night. You could do it weekly, monthly, or take a weekend away. Whatever you do, make sure you're doing something you'll both enjoy because this is about strengthening your relationship and working on the bond that brought you together in the first place.

Now, date night is an awesome idea. However, planning it together is much better. Create some fun while you're at it—try different places, cuisines, and so on. If you keep going to the same place all the time, the routine might kill the romance you're trying to rekindle.

## Tech-Free Spaces

Identify sections of your home that should be free from tech. A good place to start is the bedroom. This is a rule you should enforce strictly. You could also get a third phone where people can reach you in the event of emergencies when both of your devices are turned off for the night. Share this with your kids, close friends, family members, or anyone else you feel deserves the right to have priority access to you on an emergency basis.

## Shared Routines

Amid your busy day, find a way to align your routines so that you can do things together. Don't just end up sharing things, be intentional about it. For example, shower together, go for evening walks, use the same car to get to work, if possible, or share a part of your commute together. These things remind you of the important person in your life, and usually give you something to look forward to at the end of the day.

## The Power of Surprises

When was the last time you surprised your spouse or woke up to a lovely surprise? Surprises are common in the dating phase or the earlier stages of relationships. Beyond that, we let things go and take each other for granted. There are lots of surprises that could bring life back into your relationship. Here are some ideas you could explore:

- Plan an activity that's different from your regular routine. The point here is to infuse some spontaneity into the relationship.

- Think of some thoughtful gestures your spouse might love. Have something special delivered to them at work—it might even be something naughty.

- Plan a spontaneous picnic or give them tickets to an event or show they've been looking forward to.

While surprises are exciting, they can only be effective when properly planned. You have to get the timing right, or it might be awkward. The best thing about a good surprise isn't even in the act itself, but the fact that your spouse realizes how much effort you put into making it a success, and into keeping it so quiet they'd never know.

Another good thing about surprises is that they create a sense of anticipation. Having pulled it off once or twice, your spouse lives on the edge, not knowing when you'll pull the next trick on them. More importantly, it also creates a sense of reciprocity, and your spouse will feel challenged to go out of their way and return the favor.

## Reconnect Through Shared Experiences

As you try to rekindle the love, passion, and commitment with your spouse, do not lose sight of the bigger picture. The goal here is to try to win the fight against the distraction caused by tech in your lives. Therefore, try to limit the use of tech as much as possible in any of the activities you choose to engage in together. You're all growing in the relationship, more mature than where you were when you initiated this conversation with your spouse. So the time is here to truly reconnect, and what better way to do that than through shared experiences? Here are some ideas you can try:

- Exit the comfort zone and try something unique. It might be something you read about, an exciting activity, a new culinary experience, or some other new adventure. Just do something neither of you has done before, but you are willing to give a try.

- Visit local attractions, new neighborhoods, or new cities to see what the fuss is all about. You can read about them online, find out the local favorites, and explore. You might just stumble on something new that will work wonders for your relationship.

- Bring out your adventurous spirit and push your limits. Try rock climbing, kayaking, hiking, or zip-lining. The adrenaline rush in these activities has a way of giving you the jolt you need to reignite your relationship and bring you closer than ever. Besides, nothing is more amazing than a shared experience of discovery and adventure, screaming your lungs out and seeing each other so unhinged and ready to embrace whatever the world throws at you.

## *Relive the Treasure*

Life wasn't always like this. Right now, you're both too busy with your responsibilities, chores, jobs, and raising kids. It all seems too much for two people to handle. However, all this is possible because we let it happen. At one time in your relationship, you had so much fun together. Make a choice and relive those moments.

Recreate the magic. Where did you have your first date? Go back to that spot and recreate that magical experience. Think about all the good memories you've created since then. Think of the difficult moments you've been through together and you'll realize that what you've been looking for has been right there in front of you.

Reliving such moments is one of the most effective ways of reflecting on your journey together, and is also a reminder of what brought you together in the first place. It awakens you to how easy it is to take each other for granted, even when you're supposed to be sharing the rest of your lives. More importantly, this is one of the easiest ways to celebrate each other and your love.

## *Relax and Pamper Each Other*

You both realize that life has been quite the rollercoaster. You seem to be jumping from putting out one fire to putting out the next, fighting battles every other day at work, at home, and with your friends and families. That's just what being an adult means. Life throws so much at you that if you're not careful, you could get stuck on autopilot, and that's when couples create unhealthy coping mechanisms.

Take a moment and relax. You both need it; you've both earned it. Plan a special time for relaxation and pampering. A spa date would be perfect for both of you. If you decide to plan a vacation or weekend getaway, prioritize something that allows you to rest and rejuvenate.

Vacations take many different forms. For example, you could travel somewhere to explore the region, or go mountain climbing or hiking. While this is still a holiday, none of those activities are rejuvenating or promote rest. Be intentional in what you seek out of your getaways, and go for it.

Get couple facials and massages. This is a relaxing time and it allows for time for the two of you to get stressful areas in your body worked on.

The goal here is to remind one another that your well-being is important, and for that reason you constantly create moments of bliss and tranquility. Besides, such activities set the tone for intimate conversations and strengthen the emotional connection with your spouse.

# Chapter 6:

# Cultivating Emotional Intimacy

*Can the purpose of a relationship be to trigger our wounds? In a way, yes, because that is how healing happens; darkness must be exposed before it can be transformed.*

*The purpose of an intimate relationship is not that it be a place where we can hide from our weaknesses, but rather where we can safely let them go.*

*It takes strength of character to truly delve into the mystery of an intimate relationship, because it takes the strength to endure a kind of psychic surgery, an emotional and psychological and even spiritual initiation into the higher Self.*

*Only then can we know an enchantment that lasts.* —Marianne Williamson

Emotional intimacy is one of the most important things in any healthy relationship. It's something that your relationship has been lacking for a while since your spouse's addiction became a problem. Losing it may also be the reason why you've felt like you're living with a stranger. Couples fight over a lot of things in relationships, from parenting to finances, or even how to handle difficult or overbearing family members. Most of these arguments aren't usually about the subject at hand, but about the inability to connect emotionally. You see, when you're emotionally on the same page, you understand one another, so when such conflicts arise, you approach them together instead of trying to bite each other's heads off. Sadly, this is a reality that most couples don't realize until it's too late.

But what does it mean to be emotionally intimate with your spouse? It's quite simple It means sharing a deep understanding with your spouse, a relationship where there's room for mutual trust, communication, respect, and vulnerability. In essence, it's a relationship where you're in sync with one another on different fronts.

Note that having this kind of understanding doesn't necessarily guarantee that you will not have conflicts from time to time. Instead, when conflicts arise, you'll handle them differently. While most couples would argue bitterly, and try to prove a point, you'll handle your conflicts respectfully. You listen to your spouse's opinion on the matter and try to understand their point of view, and they offer you the same courtesy.

This kind of understanding is quite valuable in a relationship because it makes you both feel safe around each other. Physical safety and security aren't the only things that matter, but also the fact that you create a safe environment around one another where you can express yourselves. You're not afraid to speak your mind. You don't feel intimidated by your spouse, and you can always have a healthy engagement, especially when you have differing opinions on something. A relationship where emotional intimacy thrives will always grow to greater heights because of mutual understanding and healthy communication between the spouses. More importantly, you both feel fulfilled and satisfied and are always certain you are working toward the same mutual goals.

This might be where your relationship was a few years ago, but things haven't been the same since your spouse's addiction to their devices threatened your relationship. You feel like you're living with a stranger because you suddenly cannot understand why your spouse would rather spend time on their phone, video games, or whatever other gadget you have in the house than spend time with you. The worst thing about it is that they can't even give you an explanation for their sudden change of behavior.

What you've been going through for a while is a breach of the understanding and trust on which your relationship was built. None of this happened overnight. For that reason, recultivating the emotional intimacy in your relationship will not happen overnight either. It will take some effort, but as long as you're both committed to doing better for your relationship, you'll get there.

Sure, you're hurting because of the neglect, but when you're trying to rebuild the relationship, it's always better to create room for everyone to express themselves. What's your spouse going through? How did they end up where they are? Do they even realize the damage their addiction is causing your relationship? In a way, you are both hurting, even though your spouse might not be forthcoming with their pain.

Let me take you back to the good old days in your relationship, the days when things worked flawlessly. Do any of these statements sound familiar?

- You were comfortable around your spouse and could be yourself, do and say whatever was on your mind without fear of rejection, neglect, judgment, or misunderstanding.

- You always looked forward to spending time with your spouse, sharing intimate moments with them, or just bumming around with them.

- You could express your deepest concerns, thoughts, and feelings with each other, and you'd both provide useful feedback, insight, and at times critical opinions on the topics at hand.

- Supporting each other in whatever you did was something that came naturally to both of you.

Those were amazing days, weren't they?

Today, it seems like those days are long gone, faded into distant memory, and at times you wonder if you could ever get back to that relationship. You wonder when you lost the plot, or how you became strangers in the first place.

Now, let's explore some other statements that could define the relationship you're living through right now. Do these seem familiar?

- You don't feel confident enough to confide in your spouse about important things that are happening in your life.

- You no longer feel safe enough to share your true feelings with your spouse.

- You used to share a close connection with your spouse. Today, that feeling isn't there anymore. If anything, you feel better when you're apart than when you are in the same space.

- You feel like you don't understand each other anymore. When you have a conversation with differing opinions, it feels like an argument, like someone's trying to win and shut the other down.

- You feel like other people support you more than your spouse does. They believe in you, while your spouse doesn't, or is indifferent.

For someone who's been in an emotionally intimate relationship, and who understands what it means to share a deep connection with their spouse, the statements above are painful. You know what you've had before, and the kind of life you had when you were emotionally in sync with your spouse, so it hurts to be in this position.

All is not lost, however, so do not despair. You can reignite that spark. You can work your way back to one another, and we'll explore just how you can do that.

# The Role of Emotional Intimacy in a Healthy Relationship

Even as you engage your spouse in your desire to reignite the emotional connection you once had for one another, you need to understand the reasons why this is necessary. You cannot look for something you don't know, right? Thus, if you are going to work on reigniting the fire in your relationship, you must first understand why your relationship needs it. This knowledge will help you realize what you lost, and how valuable it is to your relationship.

Being physically in sync with your spouse is one thing, but the emotional connection is what keeps the physical connection working. You didn't just start having issues in the relationship recently. You've always had issues, but you worked through them together. That's the difference between the kind of relationship you once had and what you have right now. Let's now explore the role of emotional intimacy in your relationship, from the perspective of how it helps you lay the right foundation for long-term happiness.

## It's Good for Your Confidence

When you're in a good place in the relationship, nothing stands in your way. Not even the biggest struggles in your life can break your spirit because you know in the back of your mind that your spouse is always in your corner. You ooze this confidence everywhere you go, and you're always optimistic about life. More importantly, you feel good about yourself and know that you are loved the right way. When you have this in life, nothing stands in the way of your professional or personal goals.

## Be Honest With One Another

Emotional intimacy in a relationship makes being honest with your spouse much easier. You no longer have to look forward to the end of your day so you can be with your spouse and tell them everything about your day, only to get home, start the conversation, and realize that you have to hold back some information because you're unsure of how your spouse would respond or react.

One of the greatest benefits of emotional intimacy in a relationship is that it creates a platform on which you can communicate honestly with your spouse. When you're unable to speak your truth, misunderstandings creep into the relationship. You end up fighting over simple things that normally wouldn't be a bother to you. As long as you have to hold back, communication with your spouse is disrupted, and everything goes downhill after that. When you're emotionally in the same place with your spouse, you can discuss your thoughts and feelings about everything.

## *Multifaceted Growth*

A good relationship creates the perfect environment for growth. You're both growing in the relationship and in the lives you've built outside the relationship. Emotional intimacy helps you understand that even though you are committed to your relationship, you still have independent lives that require equal attention and commitment for your overall growth.

One of the biggest mistakes a lot of couples make in relationships is that they deny each other the opportunity to continue growing and evolving independently. When you're emotionally in sync with your spouse, you both understand that the success of your independent lives is just as important as the success of the life you're building together. You might have different sets of friends, social circles, careers, and so on, and allow those relationships room to grow just as much as your relationship needs room to grow. You respect each other's spaces and appreciate the role of their independent relationships in the greater growth of your lives.

Such is the role of emotional intimacy in your lives. You're not just spouses, you become life spouses. As your bonds grow stronger, you realize every day that this is the person you want to spend the rest of your life with, and you made the right choice.

# Practicing Active Listening and Empathy

Living with someone who's lost in their tech can be frustrating. Every so often, you feel like they can hear what you are saying, but they don't honestly listen to what you're talking about. This is where you learn to practice active listening in the relationship. This helps you not just talk to one another but practice empathy while at it. Being an active and empathetic listener builds on the desire to cultivate emotional intimacy in the relationship. This is true because you are learning how to be in sync with your spouse.

There are moments when conversations get so frustrating, especially when your spouse goes on and on without allowing you a chance to speak your mind. Conversations should be two-way, but yours isn't anymore. Even worse, you know that this was never the case in your earlier relationship, but it's become a trend that manifested right after you started having problems with their tech addiction. Your conversations have become more frustrating over time, and now the effort to engage your spouse feels pointless because, at the end of the day, they'll do whatever they want. It's like they were not even paying attention to you at all.

That's the problem with a lack of active listening, and it's a challenge in many relationships, even those where addiction is not present. Most people listen to respond or react, not to understand the message. This is why they end up doing what they want, not what you asked them to do.

That real and honest communication your relationship craves can only be brought back through active listening and empathy. An active listener is someone who will try to maintain eye contact with you and listen not only to your words but also to your nonverbal cues. This is someone who will affirm your conversation and ask questions to seek clarity. They are intentional about being in your presence and are genuinely concerned about your thoughts and feelings.

## *The Role of Listening and Empathy*

Empathy is the feeling of security and warmth, and the innate understanding that you care deeply for each other. These sentiments are captured in the concept of active listening, and together they create a powerful force in your conversations, bringing you closer. Active listening and empathy go hand in hand. It's impossible to understand someone's feelings without listening to them beyond their words.

When these two are present in your conversations, you build stronger foundations. You create an environment where instead of avoiding problems, you work together to solve them. You encourage and support one another through thick and thin.

This will help your relationship in the following ways:

- You strengthen your understanding of each other's thought processes, making it easier to work together even when you hold different opinions.

- You learn to pay attention to one another and the things you each hold dear.

- You create room for optimism and positive emotions in the relationship.

- You learn how to be compassionate with each other. This is possible because you see things from their perspective and understand not just what they are going through, but also why they make the choices they do.

Even though active listening and empathy are crucial in your relationship, you must never take their presence to mean the absence of conflict. Compromise is normal in relationships but within reasonable limits. Being an active, empathetic listener doesn't mean invalidating your opinions to accommodate your spouse's. Healthy disagreements are normal in relationships, and in a way, they also help your growth because you learn to explore other perspectives.

A healthy relationship is one where you acknowledge and recognize each other's differences and figure out how to work with each other.

When you're trying to heal a relationship where trust has been broken through addiction, every effort counts. More importantly, you must both be intentional in your approach. Even as you try to rebuild the trust by learning how to be more present in your conversations and the time you spend together, remember that this is not a process that can be rushed. It will take time, but if your heart is in the right place, you will get where you want to be.

To truly cultivate the emotional connection you crave, you must both learn how to be comfortable with each other in your joy, your fears, your insecurities, and your shortcomings. At this point in your relationship, you might feel like you have to unlearn your old ways and learn new strategies to reconnect with your spouse, but it's all worth it in the long run. Be patient and kind to one another. At the end of the day, there's more to this than just learning how to listen and talk to one another, or how to be emotionally intimate. The process includes learning how to be vulnerable with your spouse once again, without fear of rejection, neglect, or any other repercussions that you might have experienced in the past.

# Chapter 7:

# Overcoming Technology Addiction

*Someone once told me, 'I heard you finally got rid of your addiction.' I smiled and said, 'No, addiction doesn't work like that. Once you have it, you will always have it. I just choose not to feed it.'*

In retrospect, I should have named this chapter the Labor of Love.

This is where you do the hard, dirty work that most couples avoid. This is the point where you make a choice to fight for your relationship, to fight for your spouse. This is the point where you confront the reality that this addiction might be a bigger problem than you may have imagined, and that you might have to bring in the big guns, call the experts.

Yet you're also aware of the fact that you're standing up for your spouse out of a deep sense of personal fulfillment, the passion you have for one another, respect, affection, and commitment to the dreams you shared. You're doing this because you're not about to let some inanimate object like technology ruin your chance at a happily ever after.

Your motivation to help your spouse overcome their addiction to tech isn't just about having them pay more attention to you. It's mostly because of genuine dedication, love, and the fact that you care deeply for them, so much more than they might realize. You understand that this addiction isn't just ruining your relationship, but it could also have a detrimental effect on other social relationships that form a part of your spouse's support system. You also realize that beyond your relationship, this addiction could ruin their lives.

Regardless of the intrinsic satisfaction that could come out of this experience, you are truly passionate about helping your spouse overcome this addiction. The personal and emotional fulfillment that comes from this shared experience is why I might have called this chapter the Labor of Love.

The pervasive presence of tech is one of the reasons why overcoming its addiction is not an easy task. Addiction to tech is quite a challenge because most people don't even realize how obsessed they are. None of this is helped by the fact that most of our lives currently revolve around tech. Therefore, in most cases, we ignore the subtleties that might have been the alarm bells or red flags—until it's too late.

Tech is useful, but it can be as harmful as narcotic drugs. Unlike some drugs, tech provides instant gratification. Once you have your phone, you can access anything you want in seconds. This is why experts believe that technology could even be a more addictive habit than most. It creates the same excitement you'd get from junk food or gambling.

The reward cycle in your brain adapts and adjusts, prioritizing your immediate needs. Picture a situation where you walk into your favorite restaurant but instead of waiting minutes to have your meal on the table, you get it in seconds. If you taste it and you don't like it, you trash it, ask for a replacement, which also arrives instantaneously. Who wouldn't want that?

Tech addiction exploits your power of choice. This is your freedom to choose what you want, when you want it, and how you want it. The fact that you exercise so much control over such choices blinds you to their detrimental effect, limiting your innate motivation to change them. In essence, while you might think that you are in control because you can choose what you consume online, technology only gives you an illusion of control. You're but a puppet, hanging by threads, dancing to the tunes of major corporations that run massive decision algorithms to influence your choices online.

In the long run, like most addictions, your spouse might require professional help. However, that doesn't mean that professional help is the only solution. We just have to put this out there to help you understand that this might not be a burden you can carry alone. There might come a time when the best solution is to see a therapist, and when that happens, it's okay.

Ultimately, the goal of treatment is to help your spouse find ways of using the tech around them in a healthy, balanced manner. It's to help them function normally in their immediate environment. Even though this might be a collaborative effort, it has the greatest chances of success when your spouse is willing and committed to getting better. This is why, before you explore the prospects of professional help, you walk the journey with your spouse as we've done throughout this book. If there ever comes a time when you have to seek professional help, do it together. Remember that this isn't about you or your spouse, this is about your relationship. This is about your family.

Helping a recovering addict is often easier said than done. It's one of those things that most people talk about, but never really know the magnitude of what lies ahead. Once your spouse is willing to take strides and overcome their tech addiction, how do you help?

Collaboration and cooperation are key in this journey. Despite this being about your spouse, it's also essentially about you and your relationship. It's about identifying the challenges your relationship is facing because of the tech addiction and working on them together.

One of the biggest challenges many people go through is isolation. Once you start the recovery journey, you almost feel like the burden is on you alone, and this creates an unnecessary element of alienation.

We discussed the need for boundaries earlier in the book, and now more than ever, you need to be very clear about them. Tech is quite easy to access, so you'll have to be firm about enforcing boundaries. At times the people around the recovering addict might accidentally encourage the very behavior your spouse is trying to overcome. Therefore, as a household, you must be mindful of how you approach the use of tech in the house, and how to enforce the healthy boundaries you discussed earlier.

You must also be aware of the fact that there's a good chance your spouse might wish to indulge more than they should, or they may sneak some access during restricted hours. Even though recovery is about getting better, the biggest part of it is about accountability and taking responsibility for one's actions. Your spouse has to own up to their flaws. You must also wake up to the realization that you have a responsibility to keep them in check when you're around them. Despite their recovery status, they are not incapacitated, so they must still pull their weight around the house. Here are some things that spouses generally do out of sympathy, that you should not do with your spouse:

- **Do not make excuses for them.** This only strengthens their resolve to find some wiggle room and access the devices they should not.

- **Do not lie for them.** An addict is an addict. It doesn't matter whether they are addicted to tech or drugs, most addicts try to lie so they can get an opportunity to indulge. If you lie for your spouse, you're doing more harm for their recovery than you know.

- **Do not find reasons to justify their behavior.** Maybe they had a slip-up and got their hands on their devices while they were not supposed to. Perhaps they did it intentionally. In such a case, you must go hard on them with the consequences of breaching the boundaries you discussed earlier. Your spouse is well aware of the consequences of their actions, so if you give in and justify their behavior, you're not helping them at all. Like we mentioned earlier, accountability is one of the most important aspects of recovery.

- **Do not handle their work for them.** Everyone must pull their weight. It's a tech addiction, not a drug problem. Do not allow your spouse to laze around the house simply because they cannot access their tech and they can't think of anything else to do. Keeping them busy is a good way to get their minds off tech.

This is where cooperation and collaboration come in handy. Discuss some activities that you could engage in together or independently that can help your spouse keep their minds off their devices. Create a list of chores together and make sure everyone is accountable for their end.

I've seen a lot of couples who struggle to overcome tech addiction because as the journey gets tougher, a false sense of empathy sets in. While empathizing with your spouse is okay, recovery can only work when both of you are serious and committed to the process. You will have plenty of time for empathy, but right now, you need to do the heavy lifting. After all, there's no better way to empathize with a recovering addict than to support their recovery journey by all means necessary.

# Recognizing the Impact of Addiction on Your Relationship

How can you tell whether your spouse is addicted to their devices or if they are simply spending too much time on them? There's a difference between the two. An addict has no control over their desire to access their devices. It's like second nature to them. On the other hand, someone who spends too much time could just be indulging more than they should, but they still have that sense of control and can choose when to stop.

While the line between the two is very thin, you need to know the signs so you can start having an open discussion with your spouse about getting help before it's too late. The journey to addressing addiction often starts with understanding not just the signs, but also their impact on your relationship. It is through self-awareness that you can realize how your spouse's habits are ruining your relationship. Let's explore some signs you should be aware of.

## Behavioral Changes

One of the earliest signs of addiction is a change in behavior. You might notice that your spouse used to do or enjoy activities that they suddenly don't want to do. Instead, they'd rather spend time on their devices.

Apart from that, you could also notice a shift in the way they behave when using their devices. For example, if your spouse is compulsively looking at their devices, spending ridiculously amounts of time on their screens, or suddenly craving digital validation especially on social media, you might be dealing with an addict.

Most of these signs are not easy to detect because they're usually subtle. However, when you pay attention, you might notice how their tech use changes their approach to the daily routine and their emotional responses when things are not going their way.

## Communication Challenges

When things are not right in a relationship, you'll always notice a shift in the communication dynamics. For example, you may notice that your spouse barely looks up at you anymore when they're talking to you. You can have a conversation with them without ever making eye contact, yet this had never been the case in the past.

You might also notice that your conversations tend to revolve around virtual experiences, events happening in the lives of online communities, and so on. Your spouse might even be more informed about what's going on in an online stranger's relationship than what's happening in your relationship.

Think about your shared moments. How often are they disrupted by digital distractions? How often does your spouse break away from cuddling to check notifications on their phone? Communication doesn't always have to be verbal. You could learn a lot about the shift in your conversation dynamics by paying attention to the nonverbal cues.

## Emotional Changes

Addicts tend to behave like petulant children, throwing a fit when things are not going their way. Notice how your spouse behaves when the internet connection is down. Granted, we all get frustrated by slow or unreliable network coverage, but for an addict, things could escalate quickly.

Emotionally, you might notice a sudden shift in their mood, especially when they can't access their devices for some reason. Heightened irritability or increased stress levels are also common. Such occurrences aren't limited to the times when your spouse can't access their devices, but also when they have access, but are not having a good day. For example, if they're losing a game.

As the addiction manifests, the emotional distance continues to grow. This is the point when you take a step back, reflect, and try to understand whether the dynamic shift in your relationship could be driven by tech addiction.

## Disrupted Quality Time

Look back to the number of times your quality time has been disrupted by tech. The disruptions could be anything from using their devices at the dinner table to checking their phone on your evening walks. If you notice that tech is constantly interfering in such moments, there's a good chance that your spouse is addicted.

These are precious moments when you should be bonding, connecting with your spouse, reminiscing about the good old times, so it becomes a cause for concern when such moments are interrupted by tech.

We've only covered a few common signs of addiction from the point of their interference in your relationship. There might be many other signs of disruption in your relationship. The easiest way to recognize them is self-awareness. Once you understand the fundamentals of your relationship, you can easily tell when your spouse's energy has shifted, and identify the possible reasons why.

# Supporting Your Spouse in Their Journey to Reduce Reliance on Tech

Even though tech addiction might not be officially a mental health diagnosis, it's widely recognized as a serious problem that's disrupting relationships and lives. This is something that can happen to anyone, especially since we all use different kinds of tech these days. Once you've recognized the signs that your spouse is addicted, the next step is to support them through recovery.

How do you address this problem with your loved one? This could be a tricky one, because people react or respond differently when confronted with something like an apparent addiction. Most spouses ignore it altogether, hoping that they will come to their senses and do the right thing. That almost never ends well.

The best way to approach this and assure them of your support is to be empathetic and patient, and to encourage them to get through this. Since you've already seen the signs of addiction, here are some simple tips that could guide you in helping them get the support they need.

## *Sharing What You've Noticed*

At times the best way to awaken the reality in your spouse is to teach them about it. While you might have noticed the signs, they might not have. Your spouse might assume that the mood swings or sudden change in demeanor could be attributed to something else, not realizing that this is how their addiction manifests.

Monitor the sudden changes in their attitude and keep notes or track the frequency. Discuss this with them. Show them that these are possible signs of an addiction and encourage them to explore feasible solutions with you.

# Empathetic Communication

Few things are as difficult as telling someone you love that they might have an addiction and should seek help. This is usually a difficult conversation, one that even the strongest, most resolute individuals struggle with.

One good reason for this predicament is that such conversations usually stir up emotions, which could make things awkward. There's also the prospect that your spouse could instantly switch to denial mode, creating a communication barrier.

Nonetheless, this is a conversation that must be had, so you must come up with a good plan. First, make sure the time and setting are right. No one likes to have an uncomfortable conversation when they're having a bad day. Check with your spouse if they could spare some time to talk about something that's been bugging you for a while. You could even ask them to create time in their schedule for a serious conversation.

Prepare the conversation setting by removing distractions from the scene. Ask the kids to go and play outside, or have someone look after them for a while. Turn off unnecessary electronics like the loud music or the TV. The point here is to declutter the space so that you can both focus on each other.

Create a plan for the conversation. What do you want to address? How do you want to approach it? Do you feel this is an issue that you can tackle together, or should you suggest professional help right away? This is quite an uncomfortable conversation, so the last thing you want to do is wing it.

As you engage your spouse about their addiction, allow them space to respond and explore the issue together. Be honest and tell them that you're worried about their addiction. Here are other things that you should consider while talking to your spouse:

- Focus on their response.

- Try to understand their perspective.

- Show you care for them by asking questions to help you understand their point of view.

- Encourage them to elaborate on their responses.

Try to keep your emotions in check, because at the end of the day, this conversation is about them. Be positive throughout, and remind your spouse that you're walking this journey with them.

# Seeking Professional Help and Resources

Despite all the support you've offered your spouse, you may reach a time when the only option is to seek professional help. There's no shame in admitting that you've tried to help but have been overwhelmed. After all, this is coming from a point of love. While this conversation has been about your spouse, this particular section is also about you.

You may feel quite disheartened when you try to help someone but can't get through to them. This doesn't mean you have failed, so don't be hard on yourself. Your initiative was just one of many possible solutions that you could seek. When you need external expertise and guidance, don't be afraid to ask for it. It's the bravest thing you can do for your spouse, and your relationship. Let's explore how to go about it.

## *Embrace Your Reality*

Beating yourself up because all your efforts to help your spouse proved futile is useless. Acknowledge the fact that despite giving it your best shot, recovery is a personal initiative. Your spouse has to choose to want to be better. If they are truly committed to the well-being of your relationship, this is a good time to explore the prospect of seeking professional help.

## Discuss Options

Research professional support in your area with them. This could be anything from support groups to counselors and therapists. Narrow down your search to support services that specialize in relationship dynamics and tech addiction.

## Honest Communication

Engage your spouse about your desire to seek professional help for their tech addiction. Emphasize why you feel this would be an important step, especially given the steps that you've both taken in recent times, and the outcomes. Remind your spouse that this doesn't mean you've both failed, but it's an important step that could help you address the addiction in depth, and build a stronger relationship in the long run.

## Book Appointments

The first professional you meet might not always be the best one for you. Schedule appointments with various experts to discuss the way forward. This step should be a two-person job. Do not let your spouse do this alone. Go with them, visit as many consultants as you both feel necessary.

When you go back home, discuss what you feel about the consultant, and whether you're comfortable engaging them. At the end of the day, you should choose a professional who can provide a supportive and structured environment together. This allows you to explore the depths of your spouse's tech addiction and come up with effective strategies for change.

## Do the Work

Follow the guidance according to your counselor. Possible suggestions usually include implementing specific communication techniques, engaging in some exercises, or trying out some strategies. Your willingness to do this together will go a long way in strengthening your relationship, and it will demonstrate a deep commitment to overcoming this addiction together.

For this process to be effective, you must monitor progress and engage your counselor frequently. Discuss some of the challenges you experience with both your spouse and your counselor. Your counselor will advise on possible adjustments depending on the progress you're making, and offer guidance and support through it all.

Remember, seeking professional help is a proactive step toward helping your spouse overcome their addiction and rebuilding your relationship. This is how you create lasting, positive change in each other's lives. Someday, you'll look back and remember this as one of the crucial moments that helped your relationship flourish.

# Chapter 8:

# Rekindling Romance and Intimacy

*Here it's safe, here it's warm*
*Here the daisies guard you from every harm*
*Here your dreams are sweet and tomorrow brings them true*
*Here is the place where I love you.* —Suzanne Collins

After everything you've been through together, wouldn't it be awesome to have your spouse back? To know that they're aware of the damage their addiction to tech brought to your marriage? To know they are committed to being a better person for you, your kids, and the relationship? Attempts to rekindle the romance and intimacy in your relationship will be wonderful in strengthening your connection and keeping the spark alive. Whether you've been together for a long time or are looking to revive the passion in a new relationship, this chapter will be the kick in the backside that you need.

The art of romance has taken a beating over the years, especially in the digital age. One of the challenges of the digital world is the urgency. People seek quick outcomes, disregarding the beauty of delayed gratification. Romance is anything but quick. Not to discredit good ol' love at first sight, but in most cases, people take a while to warm up to someone, to fall in love with them, to appreciate the little things they do that only you seem to notice, to understand their likes and dislikes. Sharing your life with someone generally involves learning and unlearning.

When your relationship comes under attack, especially from an addiction, you have to work harder to emerge united on the other side. Both spouses have to put in a lot of effort to rekindle the love and romance because trust was broken. Sure, your spouse might not have cheated on you, but it may have felt just as painful. I mean, how could you play second fiddle to an inanimate object like their phone or video game? You might even think of it in the same light as a betrayal. Thus, when we're talking about rekindling romance and intimacy, this isn't light work. This, essentially, is rebuilding the relationship.

Unbeknownst to the spouse struggling with an addiction, their actions affect people around them in more ways than they might realize. Having taken the initiative to work toward recovery, the next challenge is figuring out how to rebuild the relationship. As we've reiterated throughout this book, this will only work when you both approach it with open minds. On top of that, you must both be willing to compromise and engage on this matter with genuine, forgiving hearts.

To understand the magnitude of the damage tech addiction could have done to your relationship, let's take stock of a few relationships around yours that might also have been affected.

## Immediate Family

Your kids and anyone else who lived with you through the addiction phase experienced the behavior changes first-hand. They witnessed how the addiction took your spouse away from the household. They witnessed the transition from the parent who used to play with the kids to the parent who would spend most of their time on their gadgets, unable to spare a few minutes to play or talk with other household members.

## Significant Other

You bore the brunt of the addiction, more than anyone else. You watched your spouse turn into someone else, something else that you could barely recognize. They became distant, and you became a stranger to them. No words can describe the emotional damage and trust issues that you had to endure during this period.

# *Friends*

Your spouse probably withdrew from some of the activities you used to enjoy with your friends—game night, the random weekends when you barbecued or shared a bottle of wine. At first, you made excuses for your spouse's absence, but then you got to a point where canceling plans with your friends was easier than coming up with another excuse for why your spouse has been too busy to have a conversation with them.

Considering all the relationships that were ruined by the addiction, rekindling romance and intimacy isn't just about working on what's best for the two of you. It's also about rebuilding other relationships that were ruined during that period. These relationships serve a purpose in your lives. They are your support system, so even as you work to get closer to one another, you must similarly find a way to rebuild them, too.

As you work on rebuilding these relationships, you must also be aware of the damage the addiction did to your relationship. This damage needs to be mended. Addiction comes with some behavioral changes that play a big role in the damage done to your relationship. One of these is trust. Perhaps you had spoken to your spouse earlier in the relationship about their addiction and they promised to change. However, you soon realized that instead of changing, they just learned better ways to hide their indulgence from you.

Depending on the level of addiction, some spouses become erratic and could even be cranky or, in extreme cases, violent when they are unable to access their devices. You've probably seen this in your spouse when the internet or power goes out and disrupts their online activities. This could be a concern because, in your opinion, it's just an outage and the system will soon be back online. However, for your spouse, this is a much bigger deal. Such experiences could have you living in fear, wondering why someone would behave like they do over something as simple as a network or power outage.

Finally, you might have to deal with your own guilt. When your spouse is withdrawn from you and deeply rooted in their devices, you may have moments when you wonder whether you pushed them to it. You grapple with the guilt, thinking you might have done or said something that pushed them farther away. This is usually a difficult and frustrating experience because you ask yourself questions you cannot get answers to. You feel like you enabled their addiction, even though it probably had nothing to do with you.

In such moments, as much as you're working toward rekindling the intimacy, you'll also need to learn how to forgive yourself and get over the guilt. You cannot be guilty of choices your spouse made. Even in the unlikely event that you might have said or done something that pushed them away, that's not how adults should solve problems in relationships. When one spouse does or says something that the other isn't comfortable with, you should sit down and talk about it. You don't withdraw into your devices. This calls for accountability and taking responsibility for the choices we make.

## Working Through Lost Trust

So, how do you resolve this? Here are some simple tips that will set you on the right path to rekindling intimacy in your relationship. Remember, this is a marathon, not a sprint.

### *Reach Out*

Perhaps the most important step in mending a relationship is to reach out to your spouse. They might not realize how important this step is for the relationship, so swallow your pride and be the bigger person. Things go a lot easier when you reach out, instead of the addict reaching out. Your spouse might be drowning in guilt, and unsure of how to approach you. Beginning the conversation shows them that you are willing and ready to get through this with them. You're extending them an olive branch, which makes it easier for them to overcome the guilt and warm up to the conversation.

## Separate the Person From the Addiction

Your spouse's addiction to their tech does not define who they are. At the end of the day, you must learn to separate the two, and also remind your spouse of the same. Your spouse might have lost themselves in their devices, so this would be a good time to remind them of the good things they've been doing that you are proud of. By separating the person from the addiction, you make having an honest conversation with your spouse much easier.

## Reasonable Expectations

Conversation won't be a one-time thing. Addiction affects your relationship in more ways than you might realize. You must be aware of this and not expect quick returns. Depending on how long your spouse has been swallowed up by their tech, you might not get your relationship back to the level you were used to for a while. Be realistic in your attempts at reconnecting with your spouse. If you rush things, you stand a good chance of overlooking crucial signs just to have your spouse back. In such a case, there wouldn't be much of a difference between what you're doing and the addiction your spouse is trying to overcome. After all, you're both chasing a high.

This isn't just about you rekindling the intimacy, it's also about allowing time for the resentment and other negative feelings that consumed your relationship to diminish. It's about allowing each other time to be comfortable enough to take the necessary steps to move forward together.

## Utmost Honesty

Be honest with your spouse, especially about your thoughts and feelings. The fact that they've been so consumed by their tech has hurt your relationship badly. Their withdrawal from activities you used to enjoy together or spending time with the kids could have done quite a number on you, so be completely honest with your spouse. The point here is to give them a true picture of where you are emotionally. This way, when you're both working on the next steps for your relationship, you come from a point of clarity, not unfounded assumptions.

## Move Forward

Opening up about your pain and explaining to your spouse how their addiction affected your relationship can be a difficult experience. However, once you have that conversation, you'll feel lighter. A heavy load will have been lifted off your shoulder.

Building on that, you must now move forward. Let go of the past. Sure, you might struggle to overlook some things that were said or some unfortunate incidents and experiences that happened during your spouse's addictive phase, but it's not healthy or beneficial to hold onto them, especially if you want to rekindle the passion in your relationship.

This doesn't mean that you'll just wipe everything and start on a clean slate. Discuss the process of moving forward. You both need to be clear on how long it might take you to let go of past events, when to let go of the guilt around the choices your spouse made, and so on. If you're truly to find your way back to each other and the romance that once flourished in your lives, you both deserve a fresh start.

## Reconnect

Commit to reconnecting with one another. The first steps are just as important as the subsequent steps. Keep in touch with one another. This is important in that it reminds you of what you might have lost, and why you need to get it back. It doesn't matter whether you spend a lot of time together or not, make a commitment to engaging your spouse as often as possible. Spend time together, do things together.

# Reigniting Passion and Romance in the Digital Age

You're finally both on the same page. You're ready to rekindle the passion and romance, but looking back, there's been so much distance between you that you don't know where or how to start. Well, why not start with something you both agree on? Too much tech in the relationship is unhealthy, so start with that. Keep your devices away and be with each other. Cuddle, talk, watch a movie, do something in the kitchen, get freaky, you name it.

Once you remove the distractions, it's easier to focus on each other and begin the hard work of rebuilding your relationship. Following are other suggestions you could explore.

## *Hold Hands*

Don't just hold hands, do it more often. Each time you're around your spouse is an opportunity to hold hands, even if it's only for a brief moment. Do it. The physical connection induces the body to release oxytocin, the calming hormone. Besides, sharing affectionate moments with your spouse is good for stress relief.

## *Thrill-seeking*

Step outside the house and feel an adrenaline rush. Take a hot air balloon ride, go skydiving, zip-lining, or scuba diving. There are lots of thrilling activities you can enjoy with your spouse that could take the pressure off and help you get closer.

## Outdoorsy Activities

Try to get creative outdoors. Have fun building a fire in your back yard. This can be a good bonding session for the entire family. Step outside and visit the local farmers' market. Pop into the nearby coffee house and sample the latest addition on their menu or grab your favorites. These might be simple activities, but the fact that you're doing them together with your spouse makes a big difference.

If you're truly committed to this process, you can find lots of activities to enjoy with your spouse, especially if you take the fun outdoors. Schedule some activities in advance. Add them on your calendars to stamp their significance. Rebuilding this relationship is a shared responsibility that you must both commit to. Essentially, the message you're sending to each other is that you value one another and the relationship, hence the efforts you're making.

Even though you might have a to-do list for things in your household like paying bills, budgeting, or planning activities with your kids, keep these issues away from the time you set to rekindle your romance. If you planned an outdoors activity with your spouse, this isn't the time to talk about the issues at home. Take this time to enjoy each other's company. You'll have time for the other things later.

By all means, all these are shared activities and suggestions. Do not let this become one person's responsibility. This should be fun, so plan it together. Share suggestions and in the long run, the planning will work well for your relationship, acting as a reminder of why you chose each other in the first place.

Finally, keep your devices away. Tech got you into this mess in the first place, so leave it outside your healing space. The point here is to create an environment where you can both indulge in each other's physical presence. Stare into your spouse's eyes, hold hands, and enjoy the moment. That's how you win your spouse back.

# Ways to Prioritize Physical and Emotional Closeness

Even as you work together to rekindle the fire, you'll identify different approaches that you can implement from time to time. The most important thing at this point is to foster stronger emotional and physical ties with your loved one. Sure, you've taken proactive steps and are doing a lot of things together with your spouse, but it's equally important to be emotionally intimate.

Many couples struggle to understand the connection between physical and emotional intimacy, especially after overcoming a struggle like the one you've been going through in your relationship. In most cases, couples tend to prioritize either physical or emotional intimacy. While this might work for a while, it's not sustainable. You can be physically in sync but worlds apart emotionally. In this circumstance, your relationship will be back in the doghouse sooner than you know.

Emotional intimacy is, perhaps, one of the most important ingredients to physical intimacy. In most cases, spouses confuse physical intimacy for emotional intimacy. This is why it's easier to pursue physical intimacy in an attempt at fostering stronger emotional connection with one another.

Being emotionally intimate means being open, honest, and transparent with your spouse about your emotions. It means genuinely expressing your insecurities, gratitude, appreciation, failures, dreams, fears, embarrassments, and anything else that's important to you. As you might already realize, you have to be vulnerable with your spouse to attain this kind of openness. Being this open with someone means exposing your true self to them. That's how you become emotionally intimate.

Physical intimacy, on the other hand, is the approach to creating a close bond with your spouse. Even though it's not the only way to be physically intimate, for most couples, it culminates in sexual connection.

Coming from a battle with tech addiction that has almost ruined your relationship, you might both struggle to be emotionally or physically intimate. This happens because the trust you shared was broken, and in some ways, you feel like strangers. You'll always have that lingering thought about whether your spouse is truly back to you or if this is temporary.

Vulnerability isn't limited to emotional intimacy. If anything, it's equally important in physical intimacy. You're exposing yourself to your spouse, so the element of trust that was broken must be repaired. True physical intimacy involves an emotional connection, so to fully enjoy each other's company, you must both let your guards down. You're not just getting intimate with your spouse, you're putting yourself in a vulnerable position, one that requires trust, acceptance, and someone who makes you feel safe.

When you're emotionally in sync, your physical connection also involves an intense emotional connection. This is where you're trying to be with your spouse, their past addiction notwithstanding. This kind of connection reassures each of you that even though you might not be out of the woods yet, you're in it together, and you'll get there.

Note that emotional vulnerability demands trust. If you trust one another, it's easier to be vulnerable in every aspect of the relationship. It's easier to see your spouse not as someone who almost ruined your relationship, but as someone who has understood the error of their ways and is trying to do better for the greater good of your relationship.

It makes sense therefore, that to regain true physical intimacy with your spouse, you must work on rebuilding the emotional intimacy. This way, you'll feel safer around your spouse, more comfortable and willing to move forward together.

Looking back at the period when your spouse was deeply addicted to their tech, you can now understand why the physical intimacy also subsided in your relationship. You felt like a stranger around your spouse, an experience that ruined the emotional trust you once shared.

Spoken words can only go so far. In a relationship, actions often speak louder, and this is where the emotional connection comes in. Gestures make a big difference in the relationship because they express your appreciation, affection, love, and care for each other. Here are some simple gestures we often take for granted, yet they have a profound transformative impact on your relationship:

- Surprise each other with small acts of kindness, for example, taking on each other's chores, a surprise breakfast in bed, or a hug for no reason.

- Actively listen to your spouse, not to respond, but to understand how they feel about what they're talking about.

- Commit regular and random acts of gratitude.

- Respect one another's personal space.

- Celebrate each other's achievements, even the smallest possible accomplishment.

- Support one another during difficult moments.

These random gestures usually work because they create a sense of security in the relationship. You feel understood, heard, and more importantly, visible to each other.

# Chapter 9:

# Improving Communication in a

# Tech-Dominated World

*Communicate unto the other person that which you would want him to communicate unto you if your positions were reversed.* —Aaron Goldman

We live in a world awash with distractions, and certainly, you've experienced the brunt of tech distractions in your marriage. One thing that holds marriages—and relationships in general—together is communication. How do you communicate openly with your spouse in a manner that doesn't feel like you're imposing on them? How do you express your frustrations and dissatisfaction openly without your spouse feeling like you're becoming unnecessarily confrontational?

One thing that's quite clear in the struggles many relationships go through is that without proper communication, things can get quite messy. Given the challenges your relationship has been through, you'll find it's in your best interest to learn how to communicate better with each other. The context of this chapter is to try to figure out the dynamics of healthy communication with your spouse. Remember that these are only guidelines and are not necessarily ground rules that apply to everyone. That's the thing about relationships. Even though you'll come across good advice from time to time, the most important thing is to figure out what works for you and what doesn't, and you can only do that with your spouse.

They say communication is the key to every relationship. You've heard this so many times that it's now a cliché, but you'd be surprised at just how true it is. Unfortunately, while most people know about the cliché, what they don't know is how to communicate with their spouses, and that's the one thing we take for granted in relationships. We assume that just because we talk, call, or send messages, we are communicating. There's so much more to communication than the spoken words. If anything, the first thing that many communication experts tell you is that while so much is spoken in relationships, very little gets communicated. Most of the actual communication that takes place in relationships happens through unspoken words, actions, and gestures.

If you're going to use the key to your relationship, then you need to know how. How do you use communication to unlock the doors to a healthy relationship? Well, there are many ways to go about it, but at the end of it all, you have to ask yourself whether your approach genuinely captures your feelings, ideas, and intentions. It's not just about listening to what your spouse says but about understanding each other's feelings and intentions. More importantly, healthy communication is a give-and-take situation. You must be as good a listener as you are a talker.

Since you're rebuilding the trust and other aspects of your relationship, here are some useful ideas that you could implement to help you and your spouse learn how to express yourselves lovingly.

## Open-Ended Conversations

Go deeper into your conversations. Don't just give one-word responses or talk about what you had for brunch. This is your spouse you are talking to; you're not filling out a questionnaire. Go deeper and try to know more about the subject you are talking about. Sure, you won't always be in the jovial mood to dig into every aspect of their day, but make an effort, and try to make the conversation a hearty one.

Look at this example:

*"How was your day?"*

This is one of the simplest questions that most couples can relate to. You could get a curt or an elaborate answer, depending on what mood your spouse is in.

Now, let's try a different approach,

*"You know, I could barely focus most of the afternoon, because I was looking forward to coming home so you could tell me about how the presentation went. I know you've worked so hard on it, so here I am. How was it?"*

While the two statements above convey the same message, the second one has created lots of room for an engaging conversation. Your spouse could engage you from the fact that you got distracted all afternoon, the presentation, the effort they put into the presentation, and so on. There's so much excitement in this conversation.

While the first statement might be clear and concise, and it works for many people sometimes, it also could be summed up with an "it went well" response, and then silence.

You can use the examples above to reflect on other kinds of conversations you have with your spouse. Even as you do that, remember that context is usually important in every engagement. While the second example is full of enthusiasm, it might not work when your spouse is visibly exhausted or looks like they've had the worst day ever. The smartest thing about making any conversation work is learning how to read the room. Be mindful, especially of each other's emotional boundaries, and you'll know how to approach each conversation with the appropriate energy.

## Nonverbal Cues

Can you sense the energy in each other's voices? Can you sense the frustration or the excitement? If you can do that, then you're well on your way to healthy communication. More often, couples hear the words, but not the attitude or the tone that accompanies them—and that's where most of the message lies. Picking up on the nonverbal cues isn't the easiest thing to do, but this is your spouse. You've been together for a while, so you probably know each other's moods well enough to detect a change in their tone. If you've been missing this, start paying more attention to your spouse. You'll notice a difference in how they speak when they're happy, frustrated, or even indifferent.

# Reading Minds

This is a common challenge in many relationships. Instead of listening, you try to read each other's minds. People often misconstrue the point about picking up on the nonverbal cues as trying to read minds. Things can get quite confusing when you're trying to understand the nonverbal cues and read your spouse's mind at the same time. Instead of going through all that, why don't you just ask your spouse what's up? It's much easier that way.

If you're frustrated that your spouse hasn't been paying attention to you, no amount of tantrums will make them see your point. Talk to them about it. Tell your spouse how you feel, or what you think. This saves you both a lot of time and energy that would have been wasted trying to guess what's going on.

# Mutual Effort

Making your relationship work takes a team effort. The same applies to communication. Take a moment and think about the most recent conversations you've had with your spouse, especially those that involved addressing issues in your relationship. How often did the words "we, you, and I" come up in the conversation? This is a simple tip that could help you understand the dynamics of your conversations.

For example, if your conversations always revolve around "you, or I", then there's a good chance you're either focused on yourself, or you blame your spouse This doesn't mean that conversations must always be addressed from the "we" perspective. Specificity is necessary in some instances, and in such cases, it's allowed.

However, in a healthy relationship, most conversations should be from a "we" perspective. While this might be difficult in heated arguments, you can usually find a way to subtly bring the conversation back to a common ground, where you address things from the point of what's good for the relationship.

If you point fingers in your conversations, you'll end up pushing one another away, and the environment around your conversations will always be hostile. In such situations, you'll unnecessarily be on high alert, yet there's no actual reason for you to be. A healthy conversation should flow naturally from one person to the other.

# Navigating Conflicts Related to Technology Use

The fact that you've overcome your spouse's tech addiction does not necessarily mean that you're out of the woods yet. It might be a while before the dark clouds stop hovering over your relationship. However, what matters is the commitment that you both made to making things work. Building on that, you also understand that you might not share the same sentiments about the use of tech, and that might even be one of the reasons why your struggles manifested in the first place.

Conflict is normal in a relationship. There's no guarantee that you and your spouse will miraculously end up on the same page when it comes to their use of tech. Don't shy away from the difference in opinion. If anything, use it as an opportunity to learn and respectfully explore each other's perspectives on the matter.

Ultimately, you're working toward creating a healthy relationship with technology. This is a relationship where you can both use your devices without interfering with the meaningful connections you share with one another and your loved ones. This is a relationship where you have healthy boundaries so you both know when to set your devices aside and when to use them without feeling guilty or neglecting your spouse.

Digital distractions will always be all around you. The secret is to try to make sure that you do not succumb to them, especially when you're meant to be spending quality time with your loved ones.

These tips·can help you address the perspective differences that might arise when you're talking with your spouse about taking the crucial steps in rebuilding your relationship:

- Be clear on the designated tech-free times or zones in the relationship. This is an important step because it allows you to have dedicated time for each other without disruption from your devices.

- Be open and honest when communicating with your spouse. Open communication allows you to address issues that might arise as you try to move past the addiction. It's also quite a healthy way to address the occasional conflicts around the use of tech in your household.

- By all means, prioritize the time you spend together. Quality time should never be compromised. Whether you're planning outings, date nights, or just cuddling and watching a movie at home, those moments should be treated with the seriousness they deserve.

- Be mindful about the use of technology in your household. Remember that even though you're working to overcome this addiction, your spouse can quite easily slide back into their old ways. When that happens, you could come up with unhealthy coping mechanisms when things get rough.

- Fight the technology scourge by exploring ways to use technology positively in the relationship. Technology can improve your relationship in lots of ways, so work on those together. It will be quite an enlightening experience.

Finally, do not be afraid of conflict. Avoiding hard interactions will only push you farther apart. Instead of working on your relationship, you'll be working on how to steer clear of conflicts. Prioritize spending time with your spouse without the interference of technology. Face-to-face interactions are a sure way to rebuild the trust you once had and make things better. Ultimately, technology can be an enhancement or a distraction in your relationship. The secret is to find a healthy balance.

# Enhance Communication Through Mindful Use of Technology

Despite the fact that you're trying to help your spouse overcome their tech addiction, tech is still an important part of your life and your relationship. It's important, therefore, that you find ways to be mindful of your use of tech in the relationship. When used the right way, tech can actually add value to your relationship.

We're essentially digging deep into how you can use technology to enhance your relationship. Look back to the earlier days of your relationship, perhaps when you were still dating. How did you use technology to spice things up? You probably shared a lot of photos, videos, memes, playlists, and so on. When used properly, technology can help you nurture intimacy in your relationship. It's all about common values and sharing the things you both love.

You can use technology, especially your phones, in endless ways to connect with your spouse, despite the struggles that you've been through recently. Here are some simple, yet effective ways that could work for your relationship:

- **Seize the day**. Why don't you get into the habit of taking photos of random exciting things you see during the day and sharing them with your spouse? It could be anything—a person, something on your desk, a phrase someone mentioned in your meeting, and so on. These are the subtle things that make your conversations wholesome.

- **"Our" shows**. Sure, you might not both have the same preferences when it comes to Netflix, but you can do something about that. Sit down at the end of the day and watch something either of you likes. You could also find something that you can both enjoy and wind the day down in each other's arms—that's if one of you doesn't fall fast asleep! It's always exciting when you get invested in the theme, plot, or even the characters in a show you didn't give much credit at the beginning.

- **Share your day**. This follows the same approach as the point above, but it's slightly different. Instead of random things you come across during the time you spend apart, share stuff that's going on in your day. Tell your spouse you're just about to get into a meeting, send a text telling them how the meeting went, nudge them that you'll be home in half an hour, and ask if there's something you could pick up on your way home. It doesn't always have to be something huge, in relationships, the small things make a difference.

Technology is quite a capable means to an end. What you need to do is learn how to be intentional in the way you use it. While you might have experienced the worst part of it through your spouse's addiction, that was on your spouse, not technology. Your spouse made selfish choices, and your relationship suffered because of that. You can both make bolder, better, and healthier decisions going forward on how to tap into the power of technology to improve your relationship.

## Strengthen Emotional Bonds Through Transparent Communication

Communication is the glue that holds your relationship together. Your spouse's addiction to tech, for example, sent a message that they had other things that were apparently more important to them than the relationship. You're working through that, and it's an ongoing process. In this section, we explore the power of transparent communication, since this can help you rebuild the intimacy and trust back into your relationship.

Remember the excitement when the relationship was still new? It felt like a scene right out of one of your favorite romance movies, right?

Every moment together was special, and life seemed so simple, flawless, and full of bliss. Despite everything you've been through, you can still have that with your spouse. To get there, however, you must embrace transparent communication.

Earlier in the relationship, you could communicate with your spouse without saying anything because you both simply knew what to do, when, and how. That's how a relationship is meant to be. The more time you spend with your loved one, the stronger your emotional bond grows, and the easier it gets to communicate so much through simple initiatives.

Transparency in your relationship is one of the easiest ways to build the fulfilling and happy relationship you've always dreamt of. This happens because transparency comes from unconditional love between spouses who support one another through thick and thin. Transparency means being open and feeling completely at ease with your spouse, such that you can be honest about your vulnerabilities. You create an environment where you both feel safe to share your thoughts, ideas, feelings, opinions, and everything else, without fear of repercussions.

When you have transparency in your relationship, your spouse is the one person you know who truly understands you. They will be help you through your deepest, darkest fears, they will be there through the overwhelming emotions, and you will do the same for them. You will share both the joys and the pains of your lives together, without ever having lingering doubts about each other.

You're in a good position because you can freely talk about your insecurities or any challenges you experience in life with your spouse. When you're transparent, you build a relationship on the foundation of spiritual, emotional, and physical intimacy. You both understand that you've been through some difficult times given your spouse's addiction, but more importantly, you have to get through that so you can continue on the journey you started together.

Try not to confuse transparency with honesty. Both are vital for your relationship, but they mean different things. Honesty means that you do not lie to one another. You could be truthful to your spouse, but withhold some information because you are unsure of how they'll respond or react to it. You might not necessarily be lying to your spouse, but the fact that you held something back means that you have reason to believe that opening up might not be a good idea. In essence, honesty is an important part of transparency in the relationship, but it is not, in itself, transparency.

Finally, with tech all around you, the way you communicate with your spouse could be the solution to helping you win your spouse and relationship back. Honest and transparent communication is what most couples take for granted, but in the long run, it is more valuable than you know. Make an effort, and the result will be worth it.

# Chapter 10:

# Connecting with Others for

# Support

*Sometimes, reaching out and taking someone's hand is the beginning of a journey. At other times, it is allowing another to take yours.* —Vera Nazarian

Even though this has been a journey between you and your spouse, there's nothing wrong with calling in reinforcements. At the end of the day, you are trying to breathe life back into your relationship, so this is one of those situations where you'll do whatever it takes. It is okay to seek external support to help you deal with this issue. More importantly, this approach should come from a point of love, so that your spouse doesn't end up feeling like you're ganging up on them.

Before bringing in the big guns, you should be certain that it's necessary. Some people find the idea of an external party being privy to their personal affairs quite an intrusive experience. If that describes your spouse, then you must approach the idea cautiously. Either way, outside help could be helpful if you've tried everything possible to help your spouse see not just the error in their ways, but also the damage that it's doing to your relationship—to no avail. Everyone is suffering. You still feel neglected, your kids aren't getting the attention they deserve, and your friends and family members have started asking if everything is okay because you've withdrawn from common activities you used to share with them. At this point, no one would begrudge you for seeking external help on this matter.

Admitting that a relationship is on the rocks is something many couples find hard to do. That is usually because they feel that this is an admission of failure. You haven't failed. If anything, you've put as much effort as possible into trying to solve a problem that might not even have been of your making. Yet you're the one left bearing the weight of failure. It's not fair to you at all. However, you need to take action. You're becoming a shell of the person you used to be, and you need to win your life back.

A difficult relationship is not something that should be normalized. It is not something you should get used to. The neglect, disrespect, and mistrust will eat away at you until there's nothing left, and that's why you should nip this in the bud. Things never get better. The more you ignore them, the worse they get. Even though conflict is normal in relationships, there's so much more to this than conflict. You don't have to endure it all.

Opening up to someone else about the struggles you are experiencing in your relationship might be daunting, but this is a bold step that must be taken. One thing about bringing in external help is that you can never truly tell how things will go, and that scares a lot of couples to the point where they'd rather keep their heads buried in the sand than tackle the issues that hound their relationship.

As you prepare to take this bold step, you must also understand that there's no guarantee your spouse will commit to it. Generally, it's quite beneficial if you could both be present for such engagements, but it's not mandatory. Talking to someone else could still be helpful to you, even if your spouse isn't keen on being a part of the conversation.

An alarming number of marriages end up in divorce or separation, circumstances that in some cases could have been avoided. Given the grim prospects, it might be good for you to both seek the help of an external party who hopefully can help you mend your relationship before it's too late. How do you know it's time to talk to someone? Here are some telltale signs.

## Communication Breakdown

No one knows your spouse better than you do. No one fully understands the seismic shift in the way you used to communicate at the start of the relationship compared to what happens in your home today. You're probably going days without talking to one another or exchanging only short messages, usually limited to instructions. You're arguing all the time, even over subtle things that you never used to argue about.

When you're living with a spouse who seems to prefer spending time on their devices than with you, verbal communication is but a tip of the iceberg. The loudest form of communication is in the lack of appreciation you feel. You're neglected, undervalued, and you barely recognize the person you used to call your everything. You don't even know how or what they feel emotionally. At this point, you're barely communicating as a couple, and you need to get help.

## Broken Trust

We usually equate broken trust to a spouse having an affair. While that might be the case in many relationships, it's not the only way your spouse can lose your trust. Deception is one key trust-breaker that kills many relationships, and it's quite common when dealing with addiction.

A spouse who's addicted to their devices will try to sneak away to indulge without the burden of prying eyes. They do this consciously, especially after you've had a conversation with them about the impact of their tech use on your relationship. You've probably followed all the steps we outlined in this book to help them understand the damage their actions are causing to your relationship, but none of that seems to work. Instead, they'd rather pretend when you're around.

This hurts, and it might even make you wonder why you brought it up in the first place. Trust is mandatory for any healthy relationship. If you feel the trust is broken, you might need to talk to someone about what you feel and how you can try to mend things with your spouse.

## You're Living Like Roomies

Relationships are weird at times. On the outside, people might see you as the ideal couple, always doing things together, holding each other's hands, and so on. You paint the picture of a perfect couple. However, behind closed doors, the story might be different. Someone is sleeping on the sofa, or you're sleeping in different bedrooms. If you share the same bed, you barely touch each other.

Such incidents are common when you've been trying to engage your spouse to seek help for their addiction, but that falls on deaf ears. When you get to a point where you can't take it anymore, that's when couples start living like strangers.

The quality time is gone, the intimacy is dead, and the person living in your house feels more like a roomie than your soulmate. If you're at that point, it's okay to talk to someone who can shed more light on your struggles. A different perspective might give you some insight into better ways of solving your issues, and that could help you reconnect with your spouse.

## For the Kids

Children should be raised in a happy, loving home. If you're at a point in your relationship where you feel like you're only tolerating your spouse for the kids, you should take a step back and reflect on what you're doing. Being in an unhappy relationship for the sake of your children never works out. In the long run, it causes more damage to the kids and your well-being.

Your children may be better off if you were living separately but happily, than if you're living together and miserable. The conflict and tension in your household can force your kids to figure out their own coping mechanisms, and in most cases, those are usually quite unhealthy.

At such a point, it helps to talk to someone whose insight could help you figure out whether your relationship can be saved or not. Through this process, you might realize whether there's still some love in the relationship or anything worth fighting for. While I personally don't advocate for separation, divorce, or any other version of walking away from the relationship, it's also futile to keep waiting for something that will never come. You have to be realistic about the prospects of your relationship, and from there, decide the best way forward, one that guarantees you peace of mind, and if you have children, one that puts their best interests at heart.

# Support From Friends and Family

If there's one thing whose value you can never underestimate in a relationship, it's the power of a healthy, reliable, and strong support system. Friends and family make all the difference in the world. Having looked at all the options in the previous section, it's clear that you need to talk to someone. You need a new pair of eyes, just in case you might be missing something or you are going about this the wrong way. In this section, we explore the possibility of bringing in friends and family to help you support your spouse in overcoming the tech addiction. Note that the emphasis here isn't just on bringing in friends and family, but building a reliable and safe support system that will hold you down through this and beyond.

Relationships can be lonely at times, especially when you are struggling with something like your spouse's addiction and you have no one to confide in. These are personal affairs, so it's understandable that you'd wish to keep them private. However, there's a reason why they say it takes a village to raise a child. This is one of those instances.

When it's you and your spouse trying to overcome the tech addiction, it feels like things are working. You are trying so hard to make things better together. However, when your spouse's commitment isn't guaranteed, it can be overwhelming. Despite all the effort you put in, you're still stuck in the same spot. It feels like nothing changed at all.

One of the biggest hurdles you must overcome is learning how to choose the right people to confide in. This is a serious personal matter; you can't keep everyone in the loop just because they are your friends or family members. Depending on the dynamics of your relationship, some friends and family members could be the poison that deals your relationship a deathly blow. So, to avoid that risk and to make sure that you only engage people who truly have your best interests at heart, here are some traits you need to look for:

- How do they speak about their spouses? If they don't respect their spouses, there's a good chance they won't respect yours either. They may air your linen to whoever cares to listen.

- Are they keen, trustworthy listeners?

- Do they have the capacity to empathize and be compassionate when addressing personal matters?

- Do they really have your best interests at heart? You can tell this from how involved they have been in your relationship since you started. The last thing you want to do is discuss such a personal matter with friends or family members who you barely talk to.

- Do they believe in the best for you and your spouse? Someone who has always prayed for and supported your success will be in a better place to offer constructive insight into your struggles than someone who's only there for the good times.

Weigh your options from both sides of the divide. If you can get concerned parties from your side of the family or friends and the same from your spouse's, it could be a fruitful conversation because it won't feel like your friends or family members are ganging up against your spouse. Put yourself in their shoes. How would you feel if the tables were turned? Even if they were willing to change their ways, this would feel like more of a confrontation than it would a consultative process with the aim of restoring balance in your relationship.

Apart from the need to help your spouse overcome their tech addiction, having a healthy support system teaches you that despite what you might feel for one another, you and your spouse don't necessarily complete each other. You cannot be the end all, be all for each other. There's a reason why humans are social beings. We thrive when we are surrounded by a healthy, loving community. We do well together through teamwork. Your relationship is falling apart because the element of teamwork has been compromised by your spouse's addiction to tech.

Even if it's not to discuss your spouse's addiction, make a habit of interacting with friends, family members, and loved ones. Accept invitations to birthday parties, attend cookouts, show up for that neighborhood get together, and so on. While it's a good idea to show up for such events, you must also understand that you can't show up for everything. Find a way to strike a healthy balance. Determine which invites are worth honoring, which ones you can politely turn down, and when you can make a technical appearance and then retreat to your humble abode.

## Support Groups and Therapy

You're making bold steps. Reaching out to friends or family members for help is not an easy thing to do. However, what happens if that fails? Perhaps your spouse was too apprehensive of the idea, or maybe you realized that while you are surrounded by people who genuinely love you, you are not comfortable discussing this problem with them. It's normal, and that's okay. Talking about your spouse's addiction with close friends and family can be quite a revealing experience, leaving you vulnerable and exposed. That's not something everyone can easily get comfortable around.

If that option fails, consider support groups and online communities that help people dealing with addiction. There are different kinds of addictions, so if you cannot find a support system that deals specifically with tech addiction, there's nothing wrong with joining one that deals with general addiction. After all, the support groups generally follow the same guidelines. You might not find a tech support group, but the local Alanon group might be quite useful.

You're not just asking for help, you're also making yourself accessible. You can learn so much from online support groups and, perhaps even more importantly, other people could learn much from your experience. In the long run, this is an invaluable experience and resource that will help you make incredible progress in winning back your relationship.

## Couples Therapy

You might also want to consider the prospect of couples therapy. Couples therapy goes by different names, including marital therapy or marriage counseling. Don't let the names intimidate you if you're still dating and haven't discussed the subject of marriage yet. The concept is simple: Your relationship is struggling and you need to figure out the root cause. Sure, you know about your spouse's addiction to tech, but that's just the biggest symptom that you can see. There might be some underlying issues that you could only unearth in therapy.

One of the reasons why couples therapy works is because it addresses a fundamental flaw many relationships go through—communication breakdown. Couples start drifting apart when they can no longer communicate on the same wavelength. As long as you can't get your message across to each other, there's a high likelihood that your relationship will struggle. The fact that your spouse is addicted to their devices is proof of that.

Ask yourself, what's so difficult that they'd rather indulge in their tech than engage you openly and talk about what's on their mind? What changed? Because there was a time when you were comfortable enough and you'd come to each other with your problems and try to seek lasting solutions. You even approached each other's problems as a unit. These days, you barely know what's going on in each other's lives. Even worse, you don't even feel comfortable or safe coming to each other with your problems.

By improving communication skills, it's easier for warring spouses to heal, have honest conversations about their differences, and commit to working on the relationship and growing together. Couples therapy can help you rebuild the trust, consideration, and mutual respect you once had for each other.

What do you stand to gain from this? Well, apart from being able to talk about your spouse's addiction in a healthy setting, therapy can be useful to your relationship in the following ways.

## Deep Understanding

You might know about your spouse's addiction, but how well do you know your spouse? We take a lot of things for granted in relationships, and these eventually lay the foundation for conflict. For example, what are the dynamics in your relationship? Who holds the most power in the relationship, and why? Is there a power balance or imbalance in the relationship? Is there a sense of resentment between the spouses? How do you handle or resolve conflict? What are the common issues you confront each other about?

The answers to such questions can give you a clearer understanding of the dynamics of your relationship. When you consider them, you'll soon realize why your spouse's addiction has manifested for as long as it has. You might even come to understand the real issues your spouse is trying to avoid by escaping into their tech. Such truths will not only heal your relationship, they'll also bring you closer and strengthen your bonds.

## Impartiality

When you're talking to your spouse about their addiction, you may at times feel like you're having a monologue, or a one-sided conversation. Those cannot be productive, given the issues at hand. Therapy gives you an impartial sounding board where you can finally feel heard without being judged.

Therapists listen to both sides of the story, so you can both trust that your opinions are valid. After listening to each of you, your therapist can provide impartial, honest, and unbiased feedback. You've probably gotten so used to the unproductive back and forth with your spouse that at times you miss the valid points each of you is making. When couples argue, in most cases each spouse is trying to deal the winning blow to the argument. That's not the case in therapy.

In fact, some therapists will even encourage you to have a go at each other the way you usually do at home so they can observe you in your natural element. From there, it gets easier to dissect the issues once you've all let out the anger and frustrations you hold over one another. That's the point where you begin to solve the real problem. A neutral party's unbiased feedback could be the difference your relationship has needed all along, but you just never realized it.

## Safe Space

Your therapist means it when they tell you that this is a safe space. As long as you and your spouse are in a conflict situation, such a space is one of the most important things you need. A safe space is one where you can speak your truth, be vulnerable without the fear of being judged or misunderstood, be honest and open up about your fears. These are things that feel quite scary when you're talking to your spouse, but not so much when you're talking to your therapist.

One thing you'll also appreciate about therapy is that inside the safe space, you learn how to set and enforce boundaries. This is an effective process because you both learn how to communicate effectively and feel safe at the same time.

## Explore Other Perspectives

It's hard to consider your spouse's perspective when you're not on the same page. It's even harder now that their addiction is wrecking your relationship. Talking to them bore no fruits so far, so you considered therapy. Therapy creates a safe space where you can both consider each other's perspectives. When you're arguing with your spouse, everyone focuses on their own feelings and their own needs.

Therapy helps you step aside from all that and consider your spouse's point of view. It's not about being selfish, but trying to get a bigger picture of why your spouse feels they are justified to be where they are in the relationship. By overcoming this barrier, therapy helps couples take an objective look at the relationship, making it easier to work back from miscommunication to getting a clear understanding of the problem at hand.

## Take Bold Steps Forward

What you're going through is no different from what other relationships experience. It's normal for couples to struggle through various issues, the only difference being that yours is an addiction problem. Whatever you need to work through, therapy can help you set the ball in motion and hopefully commit to solving the roadblocks in your relationship.

In the end, you might realize that your spouse's addiction wasn't really the problem, but an easier outlet to help them conceal the real problem that was bothering them. If you ever feel like you are not in a position to have a healthy argument or get on the same page with your spouse about something—in this case, their addiction—therapy could help you find a healthy and sustainable resolution, or show you how to take proactive steps to make the rest of your lives easier and more harmonious.

## Coping Mechanisms

Since your spouse is addicted to their tech, they can't give you the attention you deserve. They're probably using their addiction as a coping mechanism for something they're not willing to talk about yet. You might, as a result, end up creating your own coping mechanisms, which might drive you farther apart.

Through therapy, you can learn how to create healthy and strategic coping mechanisms that do not put your relationship at risk. You'll learn how to navigate the problem and put appropriate measures in place that can help you and your spouse. This ultimately takes the weight of sadness, anger, stress, and mistrust off your shoulders, paving the way for a healthy relationship. Remember that healthy coping mechanisms won't just help you find solutions to your pressing issues, but could also be useful for future challenges that might befall your relationship.

## Understand Where You Are

At the beginning of therapy, most couples believe they know what they want out of the relationship. They believe that they have what it takes to repair and heal the relationship. However, as the conversations continue, therapy can unearth hidden truths that could change the course of the relationship. For example, your spouse might open up and admit that they no longer wish to be in the relationship. At that point, conversations would change course from the original conversation.

Therapy helps you get clarity, not just about your spouse's feelings, but also about yours. Perhaps you might be the spouse who has been feeling like walking away from the relationship instead of committing to fixing it. Counseling can make a big difference in giving you clarity instead of wandering aimlessly.

## Earn the Trust

The longer your spouse spent time on their devices, the more they lost your trust. It got to a point where you were living like strangers in the same house, indifferent to each other's presence. Trust issues, especially those that manifest through addiction, could arise from various reasons.

As you work through therapy, you can both open up about why you feel you're in a different place in the relationship, why you feel you cannot trust each other, and more importantly, how to seek or grant forgiveness and develop a process for earning back the trust. While it might be difficult to earn back trust lost in a relationship, it's not impossible. Therapy gives you the right tools with which you could start rebuilding your relationship.

## Missing the Spark

The struggles you experience before coming to therapy join a long list of things that kill the intimacy in a relationship. Think about it for a minute. You're already dealing with bills, paying your student loans, taking care of your parents or other older relatives, sibling rivalry, a difficult boss at work, traffic, high cost of living, and so on. All these things eat into the little time you have for your relationship, making it harder for couples to be as intimate in the relationship as they were at the beginning. Now if you throw your spouse's addiction into the mix, things get even more complicated because a sense of resentment also creeps in.

Through therapy, you can learn how to reignite that spark with your spouse. Many couples struggle with intimacy, especially if you have lived together for a long time. While you feel like the spark might have dimmed or diminished completely, that's not always the case. It takes some commitment to find it, and therapy creates the perfect platform for that.

# Chapter 11:

# The Way Forward: Embracing a

# Balanced Tech-Life Marriage

*Be aware of wonder. Live a balanced life—learn some and think some and draw and paint and sing and dance and play and work every day some.* —Robert Fulgham

What's the way forward? Where do you go from here?

It's been quite an eye-opening journey. Most couples don't realize how much they'll learn along the way when they embark on such an experience. At the onset, you were concerned about your spouse's addiction to tech. So disruptive was their addiction that you might have even wondered whether the relationship was worth the fight.

Right now, you're more enlightened, and not just about helping them overcome their addiction. You've also learned so much about yourself and things about your relationship that you might have been taking for granted all along. At times it takes a crisis to help couples rediscover their love and commitment to one another.

In an attempt to help your spouse overcome their addiction, you didn't just save them, you saved yourself, your relationship, your family. You witnessed the kind of growth that many couples only discover in therapy or, in worst-case scenarios, after they've gone separate ways.

The way forward is quite simple: living harmoniously with your spouse. Your relationship has triumphed over an addiction that has ruined many spouseships and lives. Celebrate this moment because it might just be the turning point in your lives.

Just because you made it this far doesn't necessarily mean that things will be smooth all the way. No! I cannot guarantee you that. Relationships are built around choices that each spouse makes. My hope, however, is that you both embrace the teachable moments that have defined your journey and commit to becoming better for each other.

You know the kind of relationship you had before your spouse's dalliance with their addiction. You know how good it felt, and you deserve to have it back. While that is true, you must both be genuine in your pursuit of the lost glory. Overcoming this addiction should not be one of those situations where one spouse holds something over the other. It is a fresh start, for both of you.

Your journey has been an interesting one, from trying to understand why your spouse is madly in love with their tech to getting them to understand the dangers that this poses for your household. Some hard truths will define the progress you make and how you move forward. One of them is that tech is, and will always be, a part of your lives. Your challenge is how to live with it without disrupting your lives like it used to.

The second truth is that you are committed to each other. As married peopole, remember your vows. Such experiences are often a reminder of just how close you came to giving up or losing everything you'd always wanted in your relationship.

As much as I cannot guarantee you that your spouse will stay the course, the same disclaimer applies to you. It's impossible to tell whether you'll stay the course. Perhaps yours is not a tech addiction, but you might have a particular weakness that could similarly threaten the peace and harmony in your relationship. So what happens next?

In a nutshell, even though this was about helping your spouse overcome their addiction, I like to think of the bigger message as an attempt at working together and mending your relationship. This isn't the first or only problem you'll face together. You'll have many more challenges down the line; that's just how life works. The lessons we've discussed through this journey don't just offer insight into overcoming an addiction. No, they are valuable life lessons that can help you and your spouse get through most challenges couples face.

That's why *balance* and *harmony* are my go-to words to sum up the next steps for your relationship. The need for balance arises in the understanding that you might not be able to control everything that happens around you. You might not even be okay with all of them. However, you both realize that there's a time for everything, and when it comes to your relationship, you have clear priorities.

Balance breeds harmony. It means learning to respect each other's boundaries. It means knowing that even though you might not be okay with some things, you understand why they might be important to your spouse. You respect their decision to engage in them, as long as they respect the shared boundaries you agreed to.

With balance and harmony, you and your spouse have an easier time sitting down and exploring the dynamics of the challenges facing your relationship without feeling like you're being attacked. You have calm, grownup conversations about interesting or concerning developments in your relationship, and this is how you move forward together, bound by your commitment to one another.

Tech is all around us, so let's go ahead and discuss how to maintain and build on the progress you've just made.

## Reflecting on Progress in Your Journey

What have you learned so far?

This has been a journey to reconnecting with your spouse, and along the way, you have learned vital lessons. It might not have been an easy journey, but one you had to take nonetheless. In this section, I'll implore you to reflect on the progress you've made along the way. Your relationship can only succeed when you're working together with your spouse. Thus, this moment of reflection calls on both of you to look back at what you might have lost, what you took for granted, what you gained from the experience, and where you want to be in the future.

At times, you may benefit from putting others' needs ahead of your own. This is the aspect of compromise that has helped many relationships thrive. Indeed, your spouse had a tech addiction that was ruining your relationship. You did realize, however, that even though you felt neglected, the addiction was a bigger problem that needed to be addressed. By focusing on helping your spouse overcome their addiction, you put their needs above your own. They might not have realized how badly they needed this intervention, but it helped in the long run. Ultimately, you gave your relationship a chance, which in the process helped to solve the neglect you were feeling.

An important lesson here is that when tackling issues in your relationship, at times it's not so much about what you stand to gain from the solution, but about what you can offer or contribute to finding the solution for the greater good of the relationship. These are the kinds of compromises that strengthen relationships with every obstacle you overcome.

As you reflect on the gains you've made through this process, one thing remains clear—you need to reconnect with the most important friend in your life, your spouse. It's quite common in long-term relationships for spouses to lose sight of one of the most important things in their lives, the strong friendship. Friendship is the foundation of many good things in life.

Couples often take their friendship for granted over the years, allowing it to be overrun by events and circumstances they experience. That warmth, the feeling of familiarity, being comfortable with one another, diminishes as other things take precedence. The obstacles could be anything from kids, illness, financial stress, family issues, or other kinds of conflict. All these are important issues that you must deal with, but we sometimes allow them to gradually dim the light of friendship. One of the greatest lessons you learn as you work through your spouse's addiction is that you can bring the shine back to your friendship.

Below are other simple, yet vital, lessons to reflect on, which you hopefully picked up through this experience.

## Actively Support Each Other

Support doesn't mean being there only in your spouse's time of need. Support also means celebrating the triumphs, however small they might be. Don't just say congratulations and leave it at that. Go out of your way and do something different for each other.

Say your spouse goes a day without delving into their tech like they used to. That's a cause for celebration. Go out for a random, unplanned coffee, ice cream, or anything else that's not in your usual routine. As you indulge, tell your spouse that you're proud of them, and their effort warrants this mini celebration. These are the subtleties that reignite the spark of friendship and rekindle the passion in your lives. These are the moments the addiction stole from you.

## Date Your Spouse Like You're Still Courting

Remember the butterflies? The excitement and anticipation throughout your day when you knew you had a date with your spouse that evening? Remember those days? Bring them back. That's another important lesson you should have picked up from this experience.

Don't just bring back the dates, go the whole mile and bring back the meticulous planning. This one-on-one time with your spouse is about your relationship, your dreams, your plans, desires, vulnerabilities, and so on. This isn't the time to talk about money, the kids, or other issues in your extended family. This is about the two of you.

Just as your spouse used to escape into their tech, you need to learn how to escape into each other's worlds. You need to go back to the days when you both knew how to turn the lights off on the rest of the world, and turn them on in your friendship. Talk to each other, gaze into one another's eyes and find that spark.

## *Rediscover the First Impressions*

Can you still remember what drew you to your spouse in the beginning? That first impression that had you wondering where they'd been all your life? Life might have gotten in the way, but those impressions are still there. You just need to rediscover them.

When your relationship is on the brink of collapse, such memories remind you of what's important, and that everything you've been looking for has been right there. Perhaps you've been rolling your eyes at your spouse's jokes over the years. You might have outgrown them, but there was a time when you'd give anything for their brand of humor.

Looking back, you'll realize that this journey was never really about your spouse's addiction to tech. That was but a symptom. This journey was about finding your best friend. It was about learning how to be with each other again, just like you were in the beginning.

# Celebrating Success and Overcoming Challenges Together

You have your spouse back. More importantly, you have your relationship back on track. This is a win, one that strengthens the bonds of your relationship. If you were drifting apart, this is the kind of win that makes you realize that together, you can achieve so much. You just need to stay focused and committed to each other and to making the relationship work.

This is one of those wins you celebrate together. However, a relationship isn't only about the good times. It's also about realizing that you can overcome your challenges together. The whole point of this section is to remind you of the need for genuine spouseship in your relationship.

Take a moment, away from the struggles you've had to overcome recently, and think of the last time you reminded your spouse of how amazing they are to you and your household. When was the last time they said something similar to you? These are the simple things that fly under the radar, yet they make the biggest difference in relationships, and in life in general.

Have you ever shrugged off your spouse when they were excited about something and trying to share it with you? Has that ever been done to you? It is such a terrible feeling, and it dampens your energy. In that moment, you wonder whether it was wise to share your joy with your spouse in the first place. Or perhaps you had a terrible day and you just needed someone to hear you out, but they shut you down instead. Such experiences make you question whether it's wise to share important things in your life with your spouse at all.

Despite all that, what's the point of sharing your life with someone if they can't be a part of such moments? We waste most of our lives looking out for the big moments, yet simple moments like these are the ones that define our existence.

Your spouse is committed to working on their addiction. It was a difficult conversation at first, but they gradually realized the damage it was doing to your relationship. It takes some maturity and confidence to get from where you started to this particular point, and for that, you should be proud. You've achieved something that many couples struggle to do. You had the option of taking the easy way out and walking away from the relationship, but you stayed put and did the work. Be proud of what you've achieved so far.

## *Where Do You Go From Here?*

You've made a lot of progress. However, you still need to learn how to celebrate success and be there for each other in the difficult moments in equal measure. Like we mentioned earlier, this is not a one-stop shop for overcoming your spouse's tech addiction. There will be challenging moments down the line. Life will throw curveballs at you when you least expect it, and when that happens, you must remember that this is not a one-person job. It takes both of you to make the relationship work. It took both of you to overcome the addiction and get to this point where you can have healthy conversations about addiction and other challenges that might be affecting your relationship.

One thing I learned in my relationship that could go a long way in helping yours is the power of gratitude. No matter what you are going through in life, you can show up and clap for someone when you're happy with your life. When you feel good about yourself, you understand that there's abundance in the universe for everyone.

You are grateful for the ups and downs because of the lessons that lie in both, lessons which make you better people, better spouses to one another. So what if your spouse has a momentary slip and sinks their attention into their devices again? That doesn't undo the progress you've made. Instead, it's a teachable moment, a reminder that you need to sit down and address the potential risks together.

Shine the spotlight on your spouse. If they have that momentary lapse, address it right away. Remind them that at this point, it's not really about the addiction, but a choice they felt they had to make. Get to the bottom of that choice with them, so you can both understand why this decision was made.

The same applies when your spouse chooses to do something with you when the easier alternative would have been to turn their attention to their devices. This is a beautiful thing, a beautiful choice. Once again, shine the light on them. Talk about how good it feels that they prioritized you over the easier alternative. Explore their thought process together. This can be quite an affirming gesture because that conversation will linger for a while.

This culture of togetherness creates a reassuring feeling of support when you're going through difficult times. It's also a reminder that you are confident in each other, and that you can handle anything that life throws your way as a couple.

# Ongoing Commitment to a Thriving Relationship

Relationships take a lot of effort and commitment to one another. All successful marriages have their fair share of challenges, but they thrive nonetheless. Success in marriage doesn't mean changing your spouse to become like you or like the version of a spouse that you want. Success depends on appreciating and embracing each other and your differences because that is what makes you who you are. That is the person you fell in love with. Ongoing commitment is necessary for the relationship to succeed because this is how you nurture it and provide it with the resources it needs to thrive. Remember that as your relationship grows, so does each of you in it.

We talk about commitment to one another all the time, but what does that really mean to your spouse? What does it mean for your relationship?

## *Emotional Intimacy and Safety*

Committing to your spouse means being emotionally intimate with them. This is bigger than physical intimacy. Emotional intimacy means consistently creating a safe environment built on trust, so you can both open up and share your deepest feelings, thoughts, and concerns. The shared sense of understanding and security will strengthen your relationship through this addiction, and through any other challenge that you might face in the future.

## *Mutual Support and Growth*

Commitment in a relationship means understanding that you can either grow together or fail together. It all comes down to the choices you make. Working together to overcome your spouse's addiction has been a great opportunity to show each other the support and mutual respect through which your relationship will grow to greater heights.

When you're both committed to the relationship, you understand that when one person is not pulling their weight, everyone else struggles. You must actively work together to achieve both shared and personal goals, and to overcome challenges together in a similar manner. Through mutual support, you both realize that you are each other's first support system.

## Security and Trust

*Trust* is one of the most commonly misused words in relationships. People often say they trust one another, but very few mean it, or put their words into action. When you're committed to each other and the relationship, you truly trust one another. You are loyal and dedicated to each other, and that's how trust grows between spouses.

When you trust someone, you feel safe with and around them. This explains why you struggled so much with your spouse's tech addiction. In those moments, you felt the trust had been broken. This is someone who had promised to give you their undivided attention, yet they found solace in their devices, leaving you emotionally wounded.

Trust is important in a committed relationship because it is also the foundation of vulnerability, and of open and honest communication. It is also what makes you know that you can rely on your spouse during difficult times.

## Shared Memories and Experiences

One of the reasons why your spouse's addiction got to you was because you were gradually losing an important part of your lives, the shared experiences. They were fading into distant memories, and once they are gone, it's usually quite difficult to work your way back.

In a committed relationship, shared experiences give you the element of safety. They could be the moments you cuddle together on the sofa, or the times when you step out for a walk, travel together, and so on.

Most of the shared experiences that make a big difference in your lives are simple things that most people probably wouldn't think twice about, yet for your relationship, they are the things you hold dearest. These shared experiences form the memories you look back to when you're away from one another. They are the memories that make you miss your spouse.

Looking at the points above, commitment to one another and to your relationship goes a long way in guaranteeing you a fulfilling and happy relationship over the long term. Your commitment to your spouse's recovery and helping your relationship overcome the challenges of their addiction takes a lot of courage. You took a bigger-picture perspective on the relationship and it worked out well for you.

Instead of giving up at the slightest hint of discomfort, you prioritized the relationship and worked through the challenges together. This dedication and investment in your relationship makes it easier for you to build a satisfying and lasting relationship because you know it takes two people to make the relationship work, and more importantly, no one is perfect.

Finally, it's important to understand that commitment to the relationship is a mutual choice that each spouse makes willingly. It's also about open and honest communication to make sure that despite whatever life throws at you, you'll always be on the same page when it comes to your relationship.

# Conclusion

No one is perfect. That, perhaps, is one of the most important lessons we can draw from this experience. The fact that your spouse is struggling with their tech addiction doesn't necessarily mean that your relationship is damaged beyond repair. As a matter of fact, you have your flaws, too, they just might not be as apparent as your spouse's.

Most relationships struggle because couples find it hard to admit imperfection. Imperfection is actually the core of who or what we are. We can't all be the same, and that's the beauty of life. It is in our differences that we complement each other. In reality, life would be quite boring if we were all the same because this would probably mean we all know the same things.

Even as you work your way through communication and other challenges that your spouse's tech use might have introduced to your relationship, I'd implore you not to lose sight of what's important—the fact that at one point in time, you committed to one another, said that you'd be there through thick and thin. You committed to reminding each other that the journey ahead gets easier when you're working together.

In the end, isn't that what relationships are about: two individuals with unique personalities coming together to achieve common goals?

Most relationships collapse not because of big problems, but because the spouses lose sight of the fundamentals or have unrealistic and exceedingly high expectations of their better halves. Thriving relationships aren't always rosy. The spouses in those relationships go through the same challenges you go through. The most significant difference, perhaps, is how they work to get to the other side of the problems they face.

Relationships are built on a lot of things. Healthy understanding is but one of the tenets of a thriving relationship. This means recognizing that your spouse might have just as many weaknesses as you do. Just so we are clear, this isn't a contest to find out which spouse brings more challenges to the relationship than the other. It is, however, a call to introspection, hoping that you understand that in a similar situation, you'd hope for your spouse to address your challenges in a loving and caring manner.

Your spouse's addiction to tech and their devices is indeed creating problems in your relationship. However, this isn't a problem that they can solve on their own. This is a problem that calls for a combined effort.

When relationships struggle, we're more often inclined to look for external reasons to try to explain the problems we're going through. Unfortunately, more often, looking inward provides the best insight. One reason why most people hesitate to look inward is because this often demands that they take responsibility for their actions.

Personal accountability is something that most people are quick to demand of their spouses, even when they find it harder to glance inward and see their role in the problems plaguing their relationship.

For the modern relationship, tech exists all around you. Therefore, it would be absurd to expect or assume that by talking to your spouse about their tech addiction, they will simply pull the plug, go off-grid, and commit to your relationship. On the contrary, this is a gradual process. If anything, it's more about rebuilding the relationship than helping them overcome their addiction to tech.

To be fair, we might even think of the tech addiction as a symptom of bigger problems. You used to do things together that you no longer can because your spouse would rather spend time on their devices than engage in those things. So, at this point, even though you're trying to help them realize the dangers of their tech addiction, the bigger message here is that you're losing touch with one another, and you need to get back to the loving spouses that you once were.

Mutual respect is crucial for the success of your relationship. It means that you see one another as equals, and you both carry the burden of making the relationship work. Neither of you should be lifting more weight than the other. At a point like this when you're buckling under the weight of your spouse's tech addiction, it's even more important to remember the value of mutual respect.

Your spouse might have an addiction problem, but as a spouse who's equally invested in the success of the relationship, you have to try to create a healthy environment to discuss this problem with them. At the end of the day, you both have a role to play in bringing back the good days to your relationship.

You must be vulnerable with one another to have a better chance of reigniting the fire in your relationship. The fact that you're willing to express your frustrations about your spouse's tech addiction is a laudable moment for you. Many people would rather ignore the problem and find coping mechanisms. Unfortunately, most of the time the coping mechanisms are unhealthy and only drive a deeper wedge between the spouses.

Don't be afraid of the outcome. Talk to your spouse. Express your frustrations, and together, you can work on rebuilding the trust you once had in each other.

Finally, I'd love to draw your attention to the importance of the individual self in your relationship. Change comes from within. You'll have an easier time improving your relationship if you understand that the change you seek must start with you. Sure, your spouse has a glaring tech addiction, but apart from the effort that you'd want them to take, what are you doing about this situation? How are you helping them realize the error of their ways, albeit in a loving and caring manner?

As much as this is about helping your spouse overcome their tech addiction, it's much easier when you also take this as a teachable moment, self-examine, and recognize your flaws in the relationship. Embrace your flaws because they are a part of you. Accept your imperfections, be kind to yourself, and more importantly, learn to forgive yourself. If you can do that, you'll be able to extend your spouse the same courtesy.

Life is a never-ending school with lots of lessons. In relationships, the lessons become apparent each day. There's no grading scheme or one-size-fits-all approach that can help you transform your relationship. However, what I can tell you is that relationships are every day. Relationships work when you commit your time and effort. Relationships work when you're open and honest with your spouse, especially about the simple things that bug you but get brushed aside.

It only takes one person's initiative to change the course of the relationship. Your spouse might be lost. Extend them a helping hand. They might be so lost that they barely realize how much help they need.

It's my sincere hope that this book has helped you turn the course of your relationship and find the love and warmth in each other's embrace that you once did.

Lots of love, and all the best.

# References

Bettelli, L. (2021, March 3). *How to talk about tech and marriage boundaries.* Grace Marriage. https://gracemarriage.com/how-to-talk-about-tech-and-marriage-boundaries

Blidy, N. (2022, June 2). *How to speak with your spouse about digital boundaries.* One Love Foundation. https://www.joinonelove.org/learn/how-to-speak-with-your-spouse-about-digital-boundaries

Brown, B. (n.d.) *Brené Brown quotes.* GoodReads. https://www.goodreads.com/quotes/823523-when-we-fail-to-set-boundaries-and-hold-people-accountable

Casey, I. (2015, February 19). *6 surprising ways technology could ruin your relationship.* Linkedin.com. https://www.linkedin.com/pulse/6-surprising-ways-technology-could-ruin-your-izzy-griffin-smith

Collins, S. (2008, September 14). *Rue's Lullaby.* Genius. https://genius.com/Suzanne-collins-rues-lullaby-annotated

Dedyukhina, A. (2016, February 14). *How technology ruins your love life and what to do about it.* HuffPost UK. https://www.huffingtonpost.co.uk/anastasia-dedyukhina/how-technology-ruins-your-love-life_b_9220128.html

de F. Szoenyi, A. (2018, August 30). *7 ways technology has ruined love and relationships.* HipLatina; HipLatina. https://hiplatina.com/7-ways-technology-has-ruined-love

de la Cretaz, B. (2020, April 16). How to get your spouse to take on more emotional labor. *The New York Times.* https://www.nytimes.com/article/emotional-labor.html

Ducharme, J. (2019, February 14). 4 digital rules you should follow when you're in love. *Time.* https://time.com/5516735/healthy-digital-relationship

Fulgham, R. (n.d.). *Robert Fulgham quotes.* GoodReads. https://www.goodreads.com/quotes/746980-be-aware-of-wonder-live-a-balanced-life---learn

Goldman, A. (2022, June 4). *56 Inspiring team communication quotes to motivate your team.* Indeed. https://www.indeed.com/career-advice/career-development/team-communication-quotes#:~:text=%22Communicate%20unto%20the%20other%20person,were%20reversed.%E2%80%9D%20%E2%80%94%20Aaron%20Goldman

Kildare, C., & Middlemiss, W. (2017). Impact of parents mobile device use on parent-child interaction: A literature review. *Computers in Human Behavior, 75,* 579–593. https://doi.org/10.1016/j.chb.2017.06.003

Levithan, D. (n.d.). *David Levithan quotes.* GoodReads. https://www.goodreads.com/quotes/793078-they-are-so-caught-up-in-their-happiness-that-they

Lucero, O. (2023). *Relationships: How to communicate when something bothers you.* Letsmend.com. https://www.letsmend.com/posts/how-to-communicate-when-something-bothers-you

Nazarian, V. (n.d.). *Vera Nazarian quotes.* GoodReads. https://www.goodreads.com/quotes/355372-sometimes-reaching-out-and-taking-someone-s-hand-is-the-beginning#:~:text=Sometimes%2C%20reaching%20out%20and%20taking%20someone's%20hand%20is%20the%20beginning,allowing%20another%20to%20take%20yours

Przybylski, A. K., & Weinstein, N. (2013). Can you connect with me now? How the presence of mobile communication technology influences face-to-face conversation quality. *Journal of Social and Personal Relationships, 30(3),* 237-246. https://journals.sagepub.com/doi/10.1177/026540751245387

Pulsifer, C. (n.d.) *55 Balance Quotes To Achieve A Harmonious Life.* trvst. https://www.trvst.world/work-skills/balance-quotes

Quinlan, A. (2018, July 26). How technology and social media is undermining family relationships. *The Irish Times.* https://www.irishtimes.com/life-and-style/health-family/parenting/how-technology-and-social-media-is-undermining-family-relationships-1.3568291

Rabinowitz, L. (2022, November 3). *How to communicate with a man that won't communicate.* Rabinowitz Counseling. https://counselorforcouples.com/how-to-communicate-with-a-man-that-wont-communicate

Reese, J. (2019, November 18). *New study shows impact of technology on relationships.* Usu.edu. https://www.usu.edu/today/story/new-study-shows-impact-of-technology-on-relationships

Sander, J. (2023). *Technology and a couple's boundaries.* Love Work Relationships. https://loveworkrelationships.com/technology-and-a-couples-boundaries

Sandoval, M. (2021). *Technology is killing romance and ruining relationships.* The Red & Blue. https://rhsredblue.com/1968/opinion/technology-is-killing-romance-and-ruining-relationships

Savarese, I. H. (2013, June 13). *How to effectively approach your spouse about relationship issues.* Goodtherapy.org. https://www.goodtherapy.org/blog/how-to-effectively-approach-your-spouse-about-relationship-issues-0613135

Sonnenberg, F. (n.d.). *Frank Sonnenberg quotes.* GoodReads. https://www.goodreads.com/quotes/tag/leadership-by-example

Timsit, A. (2019, July 31). *Smartphones are disrupting the crucial connections between parents and their babies.* Quartz. https://qz.com/1674835/technology-is-interfering-with-the-parent-child-relationship

Williams, S. (2012, May 30). *Setting boundaries for mobile technology.* FamilyLife. https://www.familylife.com/articles/topics/life-issues/challenges/media-and-entertainment/setting-boundaries-for-mobile-technology

Williamson, M. (n.d.) *Marianne Williamson quotes.* GoodReads. https://www.goodreads.com/author/quotes/17297.Marianne_Williamson?page=2

Willsky, K. (2018, December 6). *When two spouses have very different feelings about tech.* Medium. https://gen.medium.com/when-two-spouses-have-very-different-feelings-about-tech-b92f6fbddb1

Made in United States
Troutdale, OR
10/18/2024

23903030R00086